Peabody Institute Danvers, MA

3 1397 00210 7103

P9-ASF-692

101 Ways to Raise a
Happy Toddler

101 Ways to Raise a

Happy Toddler

PEABODY INSTITUTE
LIBRARY
DANVERS, MASS

Lisa McCourt

ROXBURY PARK

LOWELL HOUSE
LOS ANGELES
NTC/Contemporary Publishing Group

HQ
774.5
m33
2000

Published by Lowell House
A division of NTC/Contemporary Publishing Group, Inc.
4255 West Touhy Avenue, Lincolnwood (Chicago), Illinois 60712-1975 U.S.A.

Copyright ©2000 by NTC/Contemporary Publishing Group, Inc.
All rights reserved. No part of this book may be reproduced, stored in a retrieval system,
or transmitted in any form or by any means, electronic, mechanical, photocopying,
recording, or otherwise, without the prior permission of NTC/Contemporary Publishing
Group, Inc.

Produced by Boingo Books, Inc.

Lowell House books can be purchased at special discounts when ordered in bulk for
premiums and special sales. Contact Department CS at the following address:
NTC/Contemporary Publishing Group
4255 West Touhy Avenue
Lincolnwood, IL 60712-1975
1-800-323-4900

ISBN: 0-7373-0473-1
Library of Congress Control Number: 00-133250

Roxbury Park is a division of NTC/Contemporary Publishing Group, Inc.

Managing Director and Publisher: Jack Artenstein
Editor in Chief, Roxbury Park Books: Michael Artenstein
Director of Publishing Services: Rena Copperman
Senior Editor: Maria Magallanes
Editorial Assistant: Nicole Monastirsky
Interior Illustrations: Cheryl Nathan

Printed and bound in the United States of America
00 01 02 DHD 10 9 8 7 6 5 4 3 2 1

Dedicated to Greg, my awesome partner in this ever-evolving, often mystifying joyride we call parenthood.

—L.M.

Contents

Acknowledgments viii

Introduction ix

How to Use this Book xi

101 Ways to Raise a Happy Toddler 1

Bibliography 123

Index 131

Acknowledgments

Thank you
to Margaret and Andy Petry,
Jaimie and David Karas, Robyn and Charles Shaffer,
Julie Skokan and Mike James, Abby and Doug Zalenski,
Kathleen Cannon and Lisa and Bob Bernstein—

*for your hours of listening to details no childless person
could ever suffer through, your great ideas about everything from poop
to party favors, your skillful extraction of our children's sticky hands from one
another's hair and clothing...and mostly for your generosity of spirit in banding
together to cope with, love, and celebrate these little people the way we do.*

I hope to share this bumpy, thrilling ride with you for many years to come.

*And, of course, a special thanks to our small teachers in this course:
Tucker, Anderson, Nicholas, Emily, Ryan, Luke, Liam,
Jessica, Hannah, Cullen, and Max.*

Introduction

I am convinced that parenting a toddler is simultaneously the most incredibly fun and *most incredibly frustrating* job a human being could ever be expected to perform. No matter how much you've been warned about the "terrible twos," every novice parent secretly believes her child will be different. The first time that gut-wrenching defiance surfaces, or that first real tantrum erupts, you think, *something must be wrong. My child isn't like this. Could she have an ear infection?* But after the fourth or fifth episode, the realization begins to sink in: *my sweet, cuddly, compliant little baby is now a toddler. And everything I've heard about toddlers is true.*

Many psychologists have likened the period of toddlerhood to that of adolescence. The toddler years mark the transition from babyhood to childhood, just as the teen years mark the transition from childhood to adulthood. Both transitions are extremely difficult ones, full of conflicting drives toward independence and desires to remain dependent. It stands to reason that the toughest years for a child will also be the toughest for the child's parents.

But nature has fixed it so that parents resist hurling their toddlers out the window by making the wretched little things so unbelievably cute. And by designing them so that the horrifying behaviors are interspersed with the most heart-melting hugs, declarations of love, and adorably sweet misperceptions of the world—all demonstrating how much they need us.

Penelope Leach, a leading source of child development information and childcare advice for parents all over the world, writes,

> Children are very hard for adults to live with. In fact, the real reason everyone is so interested in early childhood discipline is not that young children are so bad but that the grown-up world finds them so tiresome. Children are noisy, messy, untidy, forgetful, careless, time-consuming, demanding and ever-present. Unlike even the longest-staying visitor, they don't ever go away. They can't be shelved for a few weeks when you are extra-busy, like a demanding hobby, can't even be ignored, like pets, while you sleep late on Sunday because they have an unfailing ability to make you feel guilty. The guilt trips that come with children are worse than the upturned cereal bowls, bitten friends or walls drawn on with lipstick.
>
> Loving children (as almost every parent does) magnifies the pain of them as well as the pleasure.

Loving them is what this book is about. Loving toddlers fully and unconditionally in spite of their many unlovable qualities is essential to their happiness. In many cases, it helps considerably to understand the reasons behind those qualities. The toddler years represent a crucial stage in a child's development. As Maria Montessori writes in *The Absorbent Mind*, "The child absorbs knowledge directly into his psychic life . . . impressions do not merely enter his mind, they form it." The impressions your child is absorbing right now are precisely that important. They are truly forming him and forming the person he will become.

I wrote this book because I wanted a good excuse to read every single thing in the world ever written about parenting a toddler. I wrote it *while* parenting my toddler, and while in regular contact with many other parents doing the same. In it, I share experiences I've had with my son Tucker and experiences of other parents. You'll also see that I've drawn heavily upon my favorite experts because I'm just a mom and they're . . . well, they're the experts. In most cases I've avoided connecting particular behaviors with exact ages since toddlers develop at vastly different rates, and the age range that is considered appropriate for reaching toddler milestones is quite wide. If something you read here does not yet apply to your toddler, it probably will eventually.

In *101 Ways to Raise a Happy Baby*, I spent a lot of pages describing the principles of *attachment parenting* (which pertain mostly to infants) because attached babies are happy babies. The same is true, of course, for toddlers. A toddler without strong, solid attachments to loving adults will not be happy. Attachment to parents provides the security and optimum framework for a toddler to develop new skills and abilities, and his happiness depends on him making these developments.

The style of raising children called *attachment parenting* offers fewer concrete suggestions for the toddler stage than the infant stage, but the important principles remain the same. First and foremost, you must know your child and accept her for the unique little person that she is. It is crucial that you maintain your close bond with lots of loving attention and time spent together. You cannot possibly bring out the best in your toddler and facilitate her happiness if you fail to form a deep, intuitive connection with her.

Listen to and trust your child. Give her the benefit of the doubt. Parenting is hard work, but it is the most significant work you will ever do. The frustrations it can bring you are matched only by the joys it can bring you. The intention behind most of the suggestions in this book is to solidify the bond between you and your child, since that bond will provide the cornerstone of your child's happiness, now and evermore. Roll up your sleeves and dig in, because your efforts to raise a happy toddler today will reward you with rich dividends forever.

How to Use This Book

Use this alphabetical subject guide to help you find quick answers to your questions. (The index will help you find more specific information.)

Behavior modification

Way 3. Replace one behavior with another. 3
Way 5. Teach sharing, but don't expect it. 5
Way 15. Use time-out to TEACH. 21
Way 16. Reconnect after a time-out. 22
Way 17. Have more than one time-out strategy. 22
Way 23. Attribute magic powers to "please" and "thank you." 30
Way 28. Expect tantrums. 35
Way 34. Don't yell! 41
Way 36. Set firm limits on television viewing. 42
Way 45. Don't rush potty time! 53
Way 46. Let him pick the pot. 54
Way 47. Figure out the best potty-teaching method for your family. 55
Way 48. Never punish for toilet-learning accidents. 57
Way 49. Demonstrate cause and effect. 57
Way 50. Demonstrate responsibility. 59
Way 52. Plant the seeds of empathy. 60
Way 59. Learn coping skills for the Destruction Zone. 69
Way 61. Stay cool in the face of embarrassing comments. 71
Way 62. Take whine-prevention steps. 72
Way 63. Don't whine back. 73
Way 70. Teach voice modulation in a fun way. 81
Way 76. Know when NOT to say "please." 87
Way 77. Give reminders to repeat offenders. 88
Way 78. Get your child to do what you want her to do 89

Bonding

Way 10. Help your toddler feel secure, daytime and nighttime. 13

Way 11. Teach your child to bond to people, not things. 14
Way 12. Don't be afraid to co-sleep. 15
Way 13. Find the best sleeping arrangement for your family. 17
Way 14. Be proud to be a toddler-nurser. 19
Way 16. Reconnect after a time-out. 22
Way 18. Help your toddler part from you. 24
Way 20. Don't sweat the tears. 25
Way 22. Model, model, model. 29
Way 25. Take toddler with you. 31
Way 29. Offer post-tantrum support. 36
Way 39. Spare the rod . . . and the sarcasm and the frightening threats. 46
Way 42. Give in to requests that "Mommy do it!" 50
Way 51. Help your child recognize joy. 59
Way 57. Give up control (sometimes). 66
Way 71. Accept offers of help, even when they aren't helpful. 82
Way 81. Let a clinger cling. 92
Way 87. Know how hard it is to suddenly be the big sibling. 100
Way 89. Read, read, read to him. 104
Way 96. Recognize a compliment in disguise. 113
Way 97. Consider skipping punishments altogether. 114
Way 98. Don't confuse "spoiling" with "giving." 116
Way 99. Listen to your child. 117
Way 100. Know your child is good. 119
Way 101. Love with all your heart. 120

Communication

Way 2. Offer choices. 2
Way 8. Don't assume *speaking* words equals *understanding* them. 9
Way 9. Know the difference between lying and magical thinking. 11
Way 16. Reconnect after a time-out. 22
Way 21. Set reasonable boundaries. 26
Way 22. Model, model, model. 29
Way 27. Learn to appreciate toddler's persistence. 34
Way 29. Offer post-tantrum support. 36
Way 30. Judge the behavior, not the child. 37

Way 31. Give directions effectively. 38
Way 33. Be understanding when you're on the phone. 40
Way 34. Don't yell!. 41
Way 40. Give reasons.. 47
Way 51. Help your child recognize joy. 59
Way 52. Plant the seeds of empathy. 60
Way 59. Learn coping skills for the Destruction Zone. 69
Way 61. Stay cool in the face of embarrassing comments.. 71
Way 62. Take whine-prevention steps. 72
Way 63. Don't whine back.. 73
Way 64. Understand your toddler's anger. 74
Way 67. Give warnings before switching activities.. 77
Way 68. Keep talking. 78
Way 69. Praise and encourage, but not too much. 79
Way 70. Teach voice modulation in a fun way.. 81
Way 75. Don't dwell! 86
Way 76. Know when NOT to say "please." 87
Way 77. Give reminders to repeat offenders. 88
Way 80. Give answers to WHY? 91
Way 86. Rally the underdog. 99
Way 99. Listen to your child. 117

Discipline

Way 6. Pick your battles. 7
Way 8. Don't assume *speaking* words equals *understanding* them.. 9
Way 9. Know the difference between lying and magical thinking. 11
Way 15. Use time-out to TEACH. 21
Way 16. Reconnect after a time-out. 22
Way 17. Have more than one time-out strategy.. 22
Way 21. Set reasonable boundaries. 26
Way 35. Discipline with forethought. 42
Way 39. Spare the rod . . . and the sarcasm and the frightening threats. 46
Way 40. Give reasons.. 47
Way 49. Demonstrate cause and effect. 57

Way 50. Demonstrate responsibility. 59
Way 57. Give up control (sometimes). 66
Way 59. Learn coping skills for the Destruction Zone. 69
Way 76. Know when NOT to say "please." 87
Way 77. Give reminders to repeat offenders. 88
Way 79. Expect testing. 90
Way 84. Don't over-condemn aggressiveness. 95
Way 85. Correct aggression CAREFULLY.. 97
Way 88. Cut off the pay-off. 102
Way 97. Consider skipping punishments altogether.. 114

Distracting toddler

Way 53. Make up songs and games. 61
Way 54. Sing and smooch your way to happier nail-clipping times. 62
Way 55. Occupy the wiggle-worm while you change that diaper. 64
Way 63. Don't whine back.. 73

Grooming toddler

Way 38. Don't be a teeth-brushing drill sergeant. 45
Way 53. Make up songs and games. 61
Way 54. Sing and smooch your way to happier nail-clipping times. 62
Way 58. Prepare for that first professional haircut. 67

Manners

Way 23. Attribute magic powers to "please" and "thank you.". 30
Way 60. Make mealtimes peaceful (sort of). 70
Way 61. Stay cool in the face of embarrassing comments.. 71
Way 70. Teach voice modulation in a fun way.. 81
Way 74. Teach your child to give and receive compliments. 85

Nature of toddlers

Way 1. Understand the toddler world.. 1
Way 2. Offer choices.. 2
Way 3. Replace one behavior with another. 3
Way 4. Make playdates. 4

Way 5. Teach sharing, but don't expect it. 5
Way 9. Know the difference between lying and magical thinking. 11
Way 18. Help your toddler part from you. 24
Way 20. Don't sweat the tears. 25
Way 22. Model, model, model. 29
Way 24. Re-learn the meaning of PATIENCE. 30
Way 26. Pretend you're as self-absorbed as he is. 33
Way 27. Learn to appreciate toddler's persistence. 34
Way 28. Expect tantrums. 35
Way 33. Be understanding when you're on the phone. 40
Way 37. Utilize the magic of water-therapy. 44
Way 43. Ban guns. 50
Way 57. Give up control (sometimes). 66
Way 59. Learn coping skills for the Destruction Zone. 69
Way 62. Take whine-prevention steps. 72
Way 63. Don't whine back. 73
Way 64. Understand your toddler's anger. 74
Way 79. Expect testing. 90
Way 82. Don't fear the fears. 93
Way 83. Fix the fear by entering its world. 94

Nursing

Way 14. Be proud to be a toddler-nurser. 19
Way 33. Be understanding when you're on the phone. 40

Parenting pitfalls

Way 7. Don't over-teach. 8
Way 15. Use time-out to TEACH. 21
Way 36. Set firm limits on television viewing. 42
Way 39. Spare the rod . . . and the sarcasm and the frightening threats. 46
Way 40. Give reasons. 47

Personal time for parents

Way 19. Take the time you need for yourself. 25

Reading

Way 89. Read, read, read to him. 104
Way 90. Take advantage of the library. 106
Way 91. Prepare your toddler for reading-readiness. 107
Way 93. Make a special book, all about your toddler. 108

Self-esteem of toddlers

Way 2. Offer choices. 2
Way 30. Judge the behavior, not the child. 37
Way 32. Encourage your budding artist. 39
Way 34. Don't yell! 41
Way 41. Honor your child's request to "Do it by self!" 49
Way 42. Give in to requests that "Mommy do it!" 50
Way 45. Don't rush potty time! 53
Way 46. Let him pick the pot. 54
Way 47. Figure out the best potty-teaching method for your family. 55
Way 48. Never punish for toilet-learning accidents. 57
Way 57. Give up control (sometimes). 66
Way 69. Praise and encourage, but not too much. 79
Way 71. Accept offers of help, even when they aren't helpful. 82
Way 72. Share the fun of your laundry. 83
Way 73. Encourage "all by self!" dressing. 84
Way 74. Teach your child to give and receive compliments. 85
Way 75. Don't dwell! 86
Way 93. Make a special book, all about your toddler. 108
Way 99. Listen to your child. 117
Way 100. Know your child is good. 119
Way 101. Love with all your heart. 120

Sharing

Way 4. Make playdates. 4
Way 5. Teach sharing, but don't expect it. 5

Sleep

Way 10. Help your toddler feel secure, daytime and nighttime. 13

Way 11. Teach your child to bond to people, not things. 14

Way 12. Don't be afraid to co-sleep. 15

Way 13. Find the best sleeping arrangement for your family. 17

Way 83. Fix the fear by entering its world. 94

Social interaction

Way 4. Make playdates. 4

Way 5. Teach sharing, but don't expect it. 5

Way 26. Pretend you're as self-absorbed as he is. 33

Way 52. Plant the seeds of empathy. 60

Way 66. Take turns. 76

Way 74. Teach your child to give and receive compliments. 85

Way 84. Don't over-condemn aggressiveness. 95

Way 85. Correct aggression CAREFULLY. 97

Way 94. Choose the right preschool. 110

Way 95. Ease the transition. 111

Way 96. Recognize a compliment in disguise. 113

Tantrums

Way 28. Expect tantrums. 35

Way 29. Offer post-tantrum support. 36

Time-out

Way 15. Use time-out to TEACH. 21

Way 16. Reconnect after a time-out. 22

Way 17. Have more than one time-out strategy. 22

Way 59. Learn coping skills for the Destruction Zone. 69

Way 84. Don't over-condemn aggressiveness. 95

Time spent with toddler

Way 10. Help your toddler feel secure, daytime and nighttime. 13

Way 11. Teach your child to bond to people, not things. 14

Way 12. Don't be afraid to co-sleep. 15
Way 13. Find the best sleeping arrangement for your family. 17
Way 18. Help your toddler part from you. 24
Way 24. Re-learn the meaning of PATIENCE. 30
Way 25. Take toddler with you. 31
Way 32. Encourage your budding artist. 39
Way 36. Set firm limits on television viewing. 42
Way 37. Utilize the magic of water-therapy. 44
Way 44. Make grocery shopping an adventure in togetherness. 52
Way 65. Stay sane while indulging your toddler's imagination. 75
Way 66. Take turns. 76
Way 71. Accept offers of help, even when they aren't helpful. 82
Way 72. Share the fun of your laundry. 83
Way 81. Let a clinger cling. 92
Way 89. Read, read, read to him. 104
Way 90. Take advantage of the library. 106
Way 91. Prepare your toddler for reading-readiness. 107
Way 92. Help your older toddler learn to write. 108
Way 93. Make a special book, all about your toddler. 108
Way 98. Don't confuse "spoiling" with "giving." 116

Toilet Learning
Way 45. Don't rush potty time! 53
Way 46. Let him pick the pot. 54
Way 47. Figure out the best potty-teaching method for your family. 55
Way 48. Never punish for toilet-learning accidents. 57

Whining
Way 6. Pick your battles. 7
Way 62. Take whine-prevention steps. 72
Way 63. Don't whine back. 73

1.

Understand the toddler world.

Toddlers are the essence of egocentrism. A toddler truly believes that everything she comes in contact with is there for the purpose of her entertainment or benefit. She believes that others can read her mind and that their job is to make sure her every wish is granted. She is fiercely driven to explore and conduct experiments to further her knowledge and development.

However, she has yet to develop the slightest tolerance for frustration so every obstacle that impedes her progress—be it a parent, her own limited abilities, or that sock that refuses to slide onto her foot—is a fair target for her wrath. Her wrath knows no bounds, as she is new at attempting to contain it. When it pours forth, it frightens her as much as it does those around her.

As a parent, it is imperative that you accept the inevitability of toddler tantrums, defiance, and aggression. These emotion explosions are simply going to happen sometimes. How often they happen will probably depend mostly on your toddler's inborn temperament. You can't completely control the behavior of another person—even your own child. But you can and should learn to control your reaction to that behavior. Your toddler will learn the ropes much more easily and quickly if you remain calm and steadfast in your teaching.

2.

Offer choices.

Once 23-month-old Tucker became very frustrated because the wind would not obey him. He knew the concept of wind and usually delighted in it, but on this day he was saying, "Wind, stop!" complete with appropriate hand gestures. That darn wind would not cooperate, and he didn't like that. But the wind was just one of the very many things he wished he could control but discovered he could not.

Toddlers want so badly to have some authority over their world. You can help them to feel a little more in charge of their lives by giving them choices whenever you possibly can. At the refrigerator, "Do you want a cheese stick or a carrot stick?" On the playground, "Do you want to go on the slide or the swings first?" While getting dressed, "Do you want to wear the red shirt or the blue shirt today?" Even at the grocery store, you can let him call some shots by asking, "Do you like this watermelon, or does this one look better?"

Just be careful not to offer a choice unless the choice is truly his to make. Don't say, "Okay, Benny, ready for your bath?" if you plan to plunk him in the bath at that moment regardless of his answer. If he says no, and you don't honor his preference, he'll feel much worse than he would have felt if you had just said, "Bath time!" Don't phrase anything as a question unless it truly is one. To ask a question and then override the answer only points out and underscores the true powerlessness of the child's situation.

3.

Replace one behavior with another.

Whenever you tell a child not to do something, try to tell her what to do instead. Then, once you get used to that, practice focusing more and more on the WHAT TO DO part. Children like to be taught new things. Tell her this is the way Mommy and Daddy do it, and then praise her enthusiastically for doing it that way. Doing so will get results a lot faster and more pleasantly than merely saying "no!"

So your little circus star wants to jump repeatedly off the back of the couch? Say, "You may not jump there because you could get hurt. Come jump off this stool instead." Say it matter-of-factly, and demonstrate a fun jump off the stool as you say it. Or your little book-lover starts ripping all her favorite pictures out of her books. If you just say, "No ripping books!" she'll go from an exciting activity to nothing. But if you say, "You may not rip your books because if you do, we won't be able to read them anymore. Try turning the pages gently, like this," you'll be providing her with a related challenge that will get her praise instead of reprimands. Say "You need to pet the doggie gently," instead of "No! Don't pull the doggie's tale!" Or "You may not pull the dog's tail because it hurts the dog, but you can pet his soft back. Doesn't that feel nice?"

Try not to use the word, "don't." Younger toddlers may not understand it, and focus instead on the rest of your sentence. When you say, "Don't stand up in your chair," she may hear a word she doesn't really comprehend, followed by, "Stand up in your chair." Instead, try to find a do-command, like "Sit down." Keep the command short and swift and very clear. Afterward, you can explain the reason for your request.

Penelope Leach writes, " . . . children find it much easier to understand and remember positive instructions than negative ones, what they should do than what they shouldn't, and much prefer action to inaction. Try to say 'Like this' rather than 'Not like that' and to say 'Yes' and 'Go for it' at least as often as you say 'No' and 'Stop that.'"

4.

Make playdates.

It's fun to get toddlers together to play and it helps them learn social skills. Young toddlers will probably not interact much and may seem not even to notice one another as they play side by side (called parallel play). While you might be anxious to see real friendships forming, enjoy this phase because it will get tougher before it gets better. Sit back with the other mom(s) and appreciate the peace while it lasts.

Once toddlers start interacting, it's not uncommon for the disturbing interactions to outweigh the adorable ones. Until your child has some practice being around peers, he won't know that they require different treatment than his parents require. He can pretty much count on you to read his mind, solve many of his problems, encourage him to play with whichever toy he likes whenever he likes, and let him sit on your head if he feels like it. It's the only kind of relationship he's known so he has no reason yet to expect his relationship with this new kid in his house to be any different.

At this point, you have the fun job of teaching some pretty big concepts like sharing, non-aggressive behavior, and respect for others. Don't expect these grand ideas to come naturally, and don't expect to be able to teach them easily or quickly. The good news is that by around age three, most kids have a pretty good handle on these social graces. Three is the age at which they will become concerned with winning friends and being liked, which will motivate them far more than your nagging did.

If your child has begun showing interest in playmates, their influence on him may be great. Kids love to imitate other kids even more than they love to imitate you. This can be a great disadvantage at times, but it can also be a big help. If you're working on potty training, invite over a child who is potty-trained and anxious to demonstrate his new skills. If you're hoping your child will show more interest in eating spinach, invite over a spinach lover. Of course, there will be times when your toddler picks up habits from playmates that you wish he'd never witnessed. Try to take the good with the bad, and realize that these influences would have surfaced sooner or later.

In *Parenting Your Toddler*, Patricia Henderson Shimm and Kate Ballen offer these great suggestions for playdate activities:

1. Tent. Drape a tablecloth over a table. Put blankets, flashlights, and some books inside the tent.
2. Easel. Tape a sheet of paper on the refrigerator and place some newspaper on the floor.
3. Large boxes. For drawing, playing store, or just crawling through.
4. Puzzles.
5. Housekeeping corner. Dress-up clothes, dolls, cars, telephones, brooms and dustpans.
6. Art table. Table and chairs with crayons, playdough, and stickers to decorate bags or cups.
7. Tape recorder. Music for singing and dancing.

5.

Teach sharing, but don't expect it.

Why are we mommies so hell-bent on convincing our darlings to share? Since most of us secretly consider our offspring an extension of ourselves, we're appalled when these little mini-me's don't treat peers with the same polite consideration we take for granted in one another. But sharing is a very abstract notion for a toddler and it will take many months of coaching before he can possibly demonstrate any skill with it.

Plan ahead for playdates by having duplicate toys, whether at your house or a friend's. Then, if a toy-squabble ensues, try to direct the toddlers' attention to the new, exciting toys you're pulling out, showing them that now they each have one of the same thing. Buy a few bottles of bubbles, some Ping-Pong balls, or a few inexpensive kites. Even cheap little party favors like horns and plastic animals can provide good entertainment. Make sure the items are identical and age-appropriate. If it turns out that the toddlers are very well-matched in temperament, you may not even run into any trouble with the sharing issue, and you may decide to save your stash for the next play date.

We have a box in our house that I take down any time a friend is over. It holds two toddler-size tennis racquets with soft, light balls, two identical trucks, Legos, blocks, duplicate little people, duplicate dinosaurs, crayons and paper, fingerpaints, sidewalk chalk, and other sharing-conducive toys. Even if you haven't prepared in advance, you could pull out two mini-boxes of raisins or pour Cheerios into two identical little cups.

Of course, in providing duplicate toys you aren't exactly teaching sharing, so as your toddler's social engagements become more regular, start showing her how to take turns. Set a timer to ensure fairness when you ask one child to give up a toy and wait her turn to play with it. If your child has toys that are new or very special to her, she will have a harder time sharing them. Put them away before her friend arrives.

John Rosemond says,

> I get a giggle out of adults who try to force two-year-olds to share. This endeavor is no less absurd than expecting a child of three to know "right" from "wrong," or a child of four to recite the Gettysburg Address. Toddlers are territorial little people. The space in front of them, and everything within it, is "mine!" Intrusions into that territory threaten the child's self-concept and, therefore, provoke distress. The more passive child cries, the more aggressive child strikes out.
>
> Sharing is one of those civilized things, like chewing with one's mouth closed, that parents are in a hurry for children to acquire. Unfortunately, children are in no equal hurry. Sharing must be taught by parents and teachers who are patient and understand that just as in learning to read or ride a bicycle, learning share is largely a matter or *readiness*.

And Shimm and Ballen, say

> Don't expect your child to hand her toys over with a big smile just because you tell her to share. Sometimes she might be willing to be the benevolent bestower of gifts, but very often she won't even consider the idea. During the toddler years, rather than chant, "share, share, share," it is more effective to

report on your child's feelings while lightly encouraging a little generosity. For example, when Annie won't share her ball with Sam, try saying: "I see you like playing with that ball by yourself. When you are finished, how about giving it to Sam. Meanwhile, Sam, here's some chalk to draw with." These words should be modified to your own style, but the idea is to translate your toddler's actions into feelings.

6.

Pick your battles.

I, personally, do not bat an eye at happy screaming, nose-picking, jumping off furniture, or carrying food around the house. To me, that's allowing a kid to be a kid. But I go ballistic at the sound of a toddler whine. So I concentrate my discipline efforts on the things that bug me most. These things will be different for every parent. The point is that you can't correct—shouldn't even attempt to correct—every little thing that might be considered misbehavior in your child. A child who is constantly nagged to reform himself will develop low self-esteem and that will make it harder for him to improve in any area.

I fled a playdate recently with a migraine from listening for over an hour to the host-child's whining pleas to his whine-indulging mother. (My only consolation was that she was probably popping Excedrin herself after witnessing Tuck's exuberant Tarzan-leaps from her coffee table.) You know what makes your skin crawl. You're the one who has to live with your child, so choose the behaviors to correct that will make for harmonious living in your home.

Penelope Leach writes,

> If you're not prepared to do whatever it takes to make a limit stick, it's better not to set it in the first place. Parents sometimes say they cannot make a limit stick when they really mean that the necessary action is too much effort. Millions of "extra" hours of television must be watched each week by children whose parents mean to limit their viewing to a particular program or time but cannot face the fuss that would result from pulling out the plug. If you aren't sure it's going to be worth your while to enforce a boundary, don't set it—even if your mother-in-law says you should. It's far better for your child's behavior (and your temper) if he is allowed to watch two hours of TV than if he is allowed to watch one and watches another that was forbidden.

> Some children do have phases when they seem intent on doing so much that's beyond the pale that parents' ability to keep track and keep calm is seriously tested. If making sure that your child . . . stays within your limits is especially demanding, set as few as you possibly can. Make sure that each one concerns an issue you really care about so that you are motivated to do everything you have to do to make it stick, and *ignore the rest.*

7.

Don't over-teach.

Your young toddler doesn't need classes. If you and your child enjoy them, by all means go, but don't feel guilty if you aren't doing it, and don't feel smug if you are. Studies have shown that classes before age three don't really make the kids better at doing things that they will easily pick up when they're older anyway. And if the class you pick is not just for fun, but is actually very instructional, your child may grow bored and resentful of your unrealistic expectations of her.

Shimm and Ballen warn,

> In the name of love, parents sometimes take on the role of teacher in order to give their toddler a competitive edge. If you find that your style is "learn, learn, learn," then you are also pressuring your child. Do you rarely read your child a bedtime story without a little lecture on the ABCs? Do you rarely let your child run freely in the playground without first teaching her to write her name with chalk on the pavement?
>
> Pushing a toddler to learn before he is ready or interested won't help him to feel good about himself or about learning. Children are so tuned into their parents that they can learn almost anything. But even when a toddler can count to forty, does she really understand the concept of numbers? For toddlers, the activity most appropriate to prepare them for reading, writing, and arithmetic is pure and simple play.

Classes can provide an enjoyable way for you and your child to socialize and befriend other mommies and toddlers. Just be sure the main focus of the program is fun, and don't schedule too many classes too close together.

8.

Don't assume that speaking *words equals* understanding *them.*

Toddlers' speech skills often develop in alarming little spurts, leaving parents astounded at the breakneck speed at which they seem to be learning things. Some children internalize concepts for some time before they begin talking about them, but others love to chatter, picking up words easily and perhaps using them at appropriate times, without necessarily knowing what they mean. In the book *Toddlers and Preschoolers*, Lawrence Kutner explains this problem with the example of a parent warning a toddler not to pull a cat's tail:

> Your child looks at you, seemingly understanding every word. He even repeats your instructions word-for-word: "Don't pull the cat's tail." Two minutes later, you hear a loud meow and a hiss, followed by your two-year-old's scream. If you are lucky, both you and your child have each learned something. Your son has learned that there are consequences to grabbing a cat where she doesn't like it. It's a lesson he'll probably long remember.
>
> More important, you've learned something about how your toddler's brain works. It's easy to misinterpret your child's behavior—especially if you're already tired or overwhelmed—as an act of rebellion or spite. (After all, hadn't you just told him not to tease the cat! Didn't he even repeat your instructions!) But that's very rarely the case. What you have here is an example of how your child's verbal and social skills have outstripped his cognitive skills—part of his normal, out-of-sync development. You've assumed things about his abilities that just aren't true.

My husband's mother told me that when she would reprimand him as a toddler by telling him to behave, he would indignantly respond, "But I AM being have! He clearly had no idea what was being asked of him. The word "behave" is far too vague.

So before you get angry and punish your toddler for his defiant behavior, take a moment to consider whether or not he truly understood your request. (Remember how tricky that word "don't" can be!) And keep in mind that even if your child does understand what you are asking of him, there will be times when his drive to do something will simply be stronger than his desire to please you. The more understanding and patient you can be with him, while gently correcting his behavior, the stronger that desire to please you will be.

9.

Know the difference between lying and magical thinking.

Though they are often accused of it, younger toddlers really do not lie. Punishing a two-year-old for speaking an untruth is futile because his goal is not deception—only a desire to create a truth where one does not exist.

We've talked about the intense egocentrism of this age child. A toddler truly believes himself the center of everything and the cause and rightful recipient of everything that he encounters. He believes himself capable of many things he can't actually do, and believes himself able to make things true by saying them.

Daddy says, "Your tricycle is in the garage," and when Daddy and toddler go out to the garage, lo and behold, the tricycle is there. By the rules of toddler logic, Daddy made the tricycle be there by saying it was.

The toddler thinks to himself, "I can say things, too." So the next time he wants something to be true, he says it as if it is.

When you angrily ask him, "Did you bite your sister?" he can tell by your voice that he shouldn't have. At this point, he wishes he had not bitten his sister, so he says "no" because he thinks that by saying it, he can make it true. In his sudden realization that you're not a fan of biting, he may actually believe that his "no" answer will please you more than a "yes" answer, without understanding that adults value the truth over getting the response they want to hear. In his mind, he has turned your question into "Should you have bitten your sister?" and by saying "no" he is only trying to get the answer right.

Lawrence Kutner says,

> …as I write this paragraph at 8:00 P.M. on a Sunday evening, I can hear my three-year-old son talking to his mother. He's insisting in a very authoritative

tone that the children's room of our local library—one of his favorite places—is still open, and that the two of them really must visit it right now.

Arguing the point with him ("I'm sure the library isn't open this late on the weekend") would be fruitless or worse. From his perspective, he wants it to be *true*, so it must be true. Luckily, like most children this age, he's easily distractible. After acknowledging how much he wanted to visit the library, my wife asked him if he would like to cook her some dinner on the toy stove we'd made out of an empty cardboard box. He thought for a second, offered to cook her some of his plastic toy fish, and promptly forgot about the library. If, instead of distracting him, she'd argued the logic and facts of the situation, one or both of them probably would have become upset.

Often what seems like defiance is just another kind of magical thinking. You tell your toddler it's time for bed and he insists that it isn't. You feel your authority is being undermined, when his goal is simply to continue playing; nothing personal. At this stage he can't understand why a parent saying, "It's bedtime," can make it be bedtime, while him saying "No, it's not bedtime," doesn't have an equal effect.

Of course, as your toddler gets older, he will sometimes lie on purpose to avoid punishment. Don't overreact, but do let him know that he must be truthful. Just like all the other social niceties he's learning, this one may take some time. If you want to get him into a habit of owning up to his mistakes, make sure he always sees you owning up to yours. Penelope Leach explains,

Small children live in a world that's difficult for them to manage and in which they often stand accused of doing damage of one kind or another. Denying wrongdoing is therefore their most usual kind of lie and the kind that most often gets them into trouble. Your child breaks his sister's doll by mistake. Faced with it, he denies the whole incident. You are probably angrier with him for the lie than you are about the breakage.

If you feel strongly that your child should own up when he has done something wrong, do make it easy. "This doll is broken. I wonder what happened?" is much more likely to enable him to say, "I broke it, I'm sorry" than "You've broken this doll, haven't you, you naughty, careless boy." But if your child does admit to something, of his own accord or because you force it out of him, do make sure that you don't overwhelm him with anger and punishments. You cannot have it both ways. If you want him to tell you when he has done something wrong, you cannot also be furious with him. If you are furious, he would be foolish to tell you next time, wouldn't he?

10.

Help your toddler feel secure, daytime and nighttime

Maybe you've been a co-sleeper all along. Maybe you've breastfed and slept with your child from infancy right up through toddlerhood. But most parents in this country do not sleep with children because of a cultural emphasis on making a child *independent* and a mistaken notion that forcing a child to sleep alone will contribute to that goal.

The truth is that the best way to foster independence in your child is to make her feel as secure as possible throughout her infancy and toddler years. And for many children, that means sharing sleep with loving parents. While co-sleeping is not for every family, it needs to be recognized as a viable option; the taboos on it need to be lifted; and it should be especially considered if your toddler is a problem sleeper.

If you don't want to sleep with your toddler, consider letting her sleep with an older sibling. Dr. William Sears writes in *Nightime Parenting, How to Get Your Baby and Child to Sleep*, "Studies have shown that children under three sleep better sharing a bedroom rather than alone in their own rooms. Parents often report that siblings who sleep together quarrel less."

Dr. Sears also points out how beneficial co-sleeping can be to the overall parent-child relationship.

> Sleeping with your child definitely has benefits for self-esteem and discipline. Welcoming your child into the family bed or bedroom (not just "allowing" this practice) sends the message "You are a special person; we care about you at night just as we care about you during the day." Nighttime parenting, therefore, carries over into the discipline of a child. One of the hallmarks of a

disciplined child is a feeling of rightness. A child who feels right is more likely to act right.

Sleeping with your child adds another dimension to the time you spend in sleep. This sleeping arrangement allows sleep time not to be wasted time. The concept of the family bed allows so many "I care" messages to come through to your child, and you convey these messages without even saying a word.

11.

Teach your child to bond to people, not things.

If you have been practicing the attachment style of parenting, you have likely formed a strong and beautiful bond with your child. Children raised in this manner are more likely to be confident, kind, and nurturing because their relationships with the people they love are the cornerstone of their existence. And even if you did not breastfeed, wear your baby in a sling, or share sleep with your infant, it is never too late to adapt some of the principles of attachment parenting, like welcoming your child into your bed.

Dr. Sears writes,

> Is sleeping with my baby going to help him become a brighter and happier child? There are many variables which contribute to children's growth and development. However, psychologists agree that the quantity and quality of mothering does affect the emotional and intellectual development of the child.

Extending the practice of daytime attachment parenting into nighttime parenting does have long term effects on the child.

One of these effects is the quality of intimacy. Many psychologists and marriage counselors report that one of the common problems of contemporary teenagers and adults is that they have difficulty forming genuinely close and intimate relationships with another person. Teddy bears and baby bottles have helped us raise a generation of people attached primarily to material things. Sharing sleep teaches a child to be comfortable being in touch with somebody; it doesn't substitute things for people. A childhood need for intimacy that is not filled never completely goes away but reappears in later years. Psychologists report that many adult fears and sleep problems can be traced back to uncorrected sleep disturbances during childhood.

12.

Don't be afraid to co-sleep.

You may have heard the Consumer Product Safety Commission's 1999 report recommending that parents not allow their children under age two in their beds. The eight-year study found 515 deaths of babies in adult beds, with 121 of them attributed to a parent, caregiver, or sibling rolling on top of or against the baby. More than three quarters of the babies smothered were infants under three months old. The other 394 deaths were due to suffocation when a baby's head became wedged between the mattress and a wall or when a baby was placed face-down on a waterbed mattress, or due to strangulation when babies fell through bed rails.

Horrifying as these facts are, they were reported completely out of context. Every co-sleeping advocate stresses the importance of parents being completely sober when sleeping with children, and also the importance of checking the bed for any potential dangers (such as waterbeds, unsafe rails, too-soft bedding, etc.). The CPSC's report fails to take into account the condition of the co-sleeping parents or the condition of the beds they were sleeping in.

What's most misleading about the ultimate recommendation is that parents hearing it will conclude that it is safer to force their children to sleep alone in cribs, when that is not, in fact, the case. In 1977 in the U.S.A., 2,705 babies died of Sudden Infant Death Syndrome. That's just one year, and that's a lot more deaths than the 515 co-sleeping fatalities the CPSC have tallied up over an eight-year period. Statistics show that the vast majority of SIDS deaths occur when babies are sleeping alone in their cribs. (The many studies conducted by James J. McKenna, a biological anthropologist at Notre Dame, have demonstrated that sleeping next to a baby dramatically lowers the incidence of SIDS.)

The New Yorker magazine ran an article commenting on the CPSC's verdict, in which John Seabrook writes,

> What makes the commission's report particularly obnoxious is that Americans are prone to believe the advice of institutional authorities when it comes to parenting. And sleep is, of all the issues new parents face, the most complex. A 1995 study conducted in the Boston area by Sara Harkness, Charles Super, and Constance Keefer found that more parents seek advice on how to get their children to sleep than on any other health or behavioral subject. Science, culture, and gender politics all play a role in the discussion—matters that are hard enough to think about when you're rested, let alone when you're sleep-deprived.

13.

Find the best sleeping arrangement for your family.

Do you consider your toddler's sleeping habits problematic? Are you forcing him to sleep alone because you think that's what's best for him, when you know in your heart that the whole family would sleep a lot better if he were in your bed? What are you waiting for—permission from Dr. Ferber? If so, read on.

What works for your neighbors might not work for you. This is true in matters of toddler-feeding, toilet-learning, and also in sleeping. Our culture has become obsessed with the popular sleep-training regimen outlined in Dr. Richard Ferber's best-selling book, *Solve Your Child's Sleep Problems*, but even Dr. Ferber himself seems to be concerned that readers have taken his suggestions a bit too far. In an interview for *The New Yorker*, he tells John Seabrook that he doesn't like the word, "Ferberize," which has become common parenting lingo for his method of training children to sleep alone. Dr. Ferber says,

> "It's like a diet…It makes it seem like that's all my work is about—that chart—whereas the whole purpose of our work here at the center is to come up with a solution that is right for each child's sleep problem. When you look at a sleep problem, you have to take everything into account—the age of the child, the sleeping situation, the parents, whether the bedrooms are next to each other. There are situations where that chart works, but it doesn't work for everyone. When I get a letter that says, 'We've been using your technique for six weeks and he cries all night'—I think that's horrible. That's very cruel."

Dr. Ferber is the guru most often cited by parents who believe that sleeping with their offspring would be detrimental to the children's welfare. In *Solve Your Child's Sleep Problems*, he writes, "Although taking your child into bed with you for a night or two may be reasonable if he is ill or very upset about something, for the most part this is not a good idea." And, "Sleeping alone is an important part of his learning to be able to separate from you without anxiety and to see himself as an independent individual."

But when John Seabrook questioned him about those statements, Dr. Ferber replied,

> "I wish I hadn't written those sentences…That came out of some of the existing literature. It is a blanket statement that is just not right. There's plenty of examples of co-sleeping where it works out just fine. My feeling now is that children can sleep with or without their parents. What's really important is that the parents work out what they want to do."

So if it was permission from Dr. Ferber that you needed in order to feel comfortable sleeping with your child, consider it granted. Consider, too, that all the studies done in favor of co-sleeping site evidence that this arrangement benefits the child in myriad ways. On the other hand, as John Seabrook puts it,

> Not one of the anti-co-sleeping authorities gives any really compelling reasons

that kids should sleep on their own, other than the parents' convenience. Most give lip service to the notion that it is important for babies to sleep by themselves in order to develop a sense of "independence." But independence is a notoriously slippery concept: does it mean autonomy, self-reliance, or solitary confinement? And, as the co-sleeping advocates point out, sleeping alone may mean merely switching dependence from the parents to objects in the crib— pacifiers, blankets, Teddy bears, and Teletubbies.

If you did not sleep with your child during his infancy, perhaps he has already established a pattern of happily sleeping through the night. But if your toddler is especially fearful of the dark or his own nighttime imaginings; if he wakes frequently with night terrors, or if he seems not to be as confident and secure as his peers, sharing sleep with him might help.

If you are considering it, you might want to simply ask your child if he would like to sleep with you sometimes. Maybe he will only take you up on your offer when he really needs it. But do not make the offer unless you're sure it's something you want to do. Many parents love sleeping with their children. We've slept with two-and-a-half-year-old Tucker his whole life and although we'll be happy for him when he decides to move into his big-boy bed, we've loved this period of closeness with him.

In that article for *The New Yorker*, John Seabrook talks wistfully about the day his son will eventually move into his own bed:

> . . . what I would miss is the sight of my son's face just as he is waking up. First comes that moment of balance between sleep and wakefulness, when the nighttime visions are fading from his eyes (does he know he's been dreaming?) but nothing like real wakefulness has registered yet. And then there is the smile, a big radiant grin provoked by nothing more than the mere presence of another day. It is remarkable to see a person

wake up with a big smile on his face each day—even if it is way too early in the morning. I'm trying to figure out how he does it.

14.

Be proud to be a toddler-nurser.

If you are still nursing your toddler, you may be feeling pressure to wean. In our society a mother who nurses her child beyond the first year is an oddity, but this attitude is neither shared by most of the world's people, nor is it in the best interest of our collective offspring.

While there are plenty of cultures where women nurse for five, six or more years, the global average is three to four years. So why are we Americans so quick to rush our children away from their most natural source of physical and emotional nourishment? The American Academy of Pediatrics recommends nursing for at least one year or *longer*, but somehow this message is misinterpreted by many mothers to mean than they should wean their children at one year.

In a *New York Times* article, Dr. Lawrence M. Gartner, a professor emeritus at the University of Chicago and chairman of the American Academy of Pediatrics' task force on breastfeeding, says,

> There is no contraindication to extended breastfeeding and no evidence that it causes psychological harm…The impression a number of us have from seeing a large number of children breastfeed for two or three years is that, if anything, they are more self-confident and can handle crowds and people well.

Perhaps mothers wean so early because they feel it will free them from the restrictions breastfeeding makes on their lives by limiting the time they can spend away from their children. But after the first year, the whole nursing relationship relaxes quite a bit, making it much easier for a mother to come and go without her child if that is what her lifestyle requires. Rather than weaning, a mother could simply cut back the number of feedings she offers until she finds a comfortable middle ground that gives her access to the freedom she needs while still offering her child the benefits of a breastfeeding relationship.

The *New York Times* article goes on to describe a study conducted by Niles Newton, a research psychologist at Northwestern University, who followed a group of children who were breastfed for at least three years:

> "His hypothesis was that if you nursed a child more than one year, you would tie that baby to your apron strings," explained Ruth Lawrence, a professor of pediatrics and obstetrics at the University of Rochester and author of "Breast-Feeding: A Guide for the Medical Profession" (C.V. Mosby, 1999).
>
> But Dr. Newton found quite the opposite. Nursing toddlers blossomed into children who were more assertive, advanced physically and mentally, and more at ease in social situations compared with those who had weaned earlier.

If you have become deeply resentful of your nursing obligations to your toddler, by all means, bring the relationship to a gradual, gentle close by eliminating one feeding at a time. But if you and your child are both enjoying the close, natural bond that breastfeeding fosters, don't let pressure from friends, neighbors, or family get in the way. Some mothers just have a tendency to want other mothers to validate their own courses by duplicating them. You don't have to make other people wrong by doing what you know is right. Just smile and let everyone know that you're confident in your mothering choices. For support and advice (yes, even weaning advice), call La Leche League at 1-800-LA-LECHE.

15.

Use time-out to TEACH.

The biggest mistake parents make when using time-outs is making them a punishment. The purpose of time-out should be to remove the child from the source of the problem, to interrupt the misbehavior, and to give the child a chance to regain his composure so that he can resume the activity better prepared to behave. An effective time-out will help him learn what is expected of him and support him in his effort to control himself better.

Don't even think about putting your one-year-old into time-out. One-year-old children have no grasp on the notion of cause and effect. They won't connect the time-out with the behavior that landed them there, so they don't stand to learn anything from it. After your toddler's second birthday, you may want to give time-outs a try. Just keep in mind that their purpose is to teach, not humiliate or penalize.

When your child is misbehaving, calmly get her attention. Look her in the eyes and say, "No throwing your shoes in the living room. Someone could get hurt. Throw this Ping-Pong ball instead." Say it as if you fully expect your statement to correct the situation. It might. But if it doesn't, and the shoe-throwing continues, try, "If you throw your shoe again, I'm going to put the shoes away and you will go to time-out." Maybe the behavior will stop at this point. If it does, reward her with a proud smile. Say something like, "Thank you for being such a good listener. Want to help Mommy peel the potatoes?"

But if, in spite of your fair warning, that shoe comes hurling past your ear, take swift action. (Never give another warning at this stage or she will forever be wise to your empty threats.) Without ranting or fuming, scoop up the shoes and place them out of reach. Take her by the hand and lead her to your pre-designated time-out spot. Any chair anywhere in the house that your toddler does not normally spend time in is fine, but try to make it an area that is removed from the main activity of the household.

Sit her in the chair and sit close by but do not hold, entertain, or talk to the child. Set a timer for one minute for each year of your toddler's age (two minutes for a two-year-old, three for a three-year-old, etc.) If she gets up, place her back in the chair and reset the timer. You don't need to scowl at her to make your point. You want to stay emotionally detached, leading her to feel that the unalterable laws of the universe dictate that time-outs follow misbehaviors. You can offer a brief explanation like, "Sitting in time-out now will remind you next time not to throw your shoes."

When she's older you'll be able to leave her alone in the chair, but for now sit near her. You can't count on her to stay put otherwise. Plus, if she senses your anger AND fears you've abandoned her, she'll be too upset to reflect on the issue at hand.

16.

Reconnect after a time-out.

Sitting in a chair for two minutes may not seem like a horrible sentence to you, but it will likely be torture for your toddler, especially if she knows that you are angry with her. So use those minutes to calm yourself as well. When the bell rings, you need to let bygones by bygones. She's served her time, so don't continue to punish her by distancing yourself. If you do she will likely become so preoccupied with your withdrawal of affection that she'll forget the reason for it and the opportunity for learning anything will be lost.

Keep the big picture in mind. The reason for the time-out was not to vindicate you, but to improve her behavior the next time around. So give her a hug and a forgiving smile. Ask her, "Do you know why you had that time-out?" She'll probably be able to tell you why, but don't be angry if she can't. Just give her the answer. Then say, "What will you do next time?" and again, spell it out for her if she has trouble answering the question.

By this point she will probably need badly to reconnect with you, and will say all the right things. Act as if you have no doubt that she is now forever cured of shoe-throwing and ignoring your requests. But realize, of course, that it may take many more time-outs before that is actually the case.

17.

Have more than one time-out strategy.

Often, the only way to stop an undesirable behavior is to time-out the offender, but undesirable behavior frequently surfaces in places and situations that call for creative compromise. Think and plan in advance what you will do if you need to discipline your child while shopping, while playing in the park, while at your sister's house, etc. Realize and expect that your child will occasionally misbehave in these situations so you can avoid overreacting when he does.

Here's an example: If your toddler runs away from you in stores, you could make a rule that any running away in a store will result in a car-seat time-out. Without yelling or getting angry, pick up your child and take him to the car. Strap him in his car seat, sit in the front seat and tell him he's in time-out. He probably won't like just sitting in a car in the parking lot, and may protest vehemently. When the time-out is over, talk to him to make sure he knows what got him there. Forgive him and help him to feel better before returning to the store.

If he misbehaves in a mall, maybe a few minutes on a bench or in a department store rest room will give him a chance to regain his composure. Stay with him, of course, but don't give him your attention or he will have incentive to keep at it. The point is just to think through and have a strategy ready to implement for different situations you will find yourself in.

18.

Help your toddler part from you.

Running from you one minute and clinging to you for dear life the next, your toddler is a bundle of contradictions. There will likely be moments, or days, or even weeks during which he HATES to be apart from you. It doesn't mean you've done anything wrong or that there's anything wrong with him. It's all part of the ebb and flow of his increasing independence. Stick by his side as much as you can, but if you do need to pry him away, try not to make yourself sick over it.

If his tears at the moment of parting bring you to tears as well, he'll be even more convinced that separation from you is terribly dangerous. So even if it's killing you inside to see him so upset, paste on your happy face and wave sweetly. It may feel as though you're being callous and unsympathetic, but letting him see you cheerful really is the best way to convince him that he has nothing to fear.

Always tell him when you'll be back. He has no idea what 4:00 means, so tell him, "I'll be back after your nap and then we'll go to the park together." If you're leaving him with a sitter, make sure it's one he knows and enjoys, and try to plan a fun activity they can do together while you're gone. Tell him in advance about how much fun he'll have. My friend Lisa made a video of she and her husband reading their son's favorite stories and talking to him. The babysitter would pop it in whenever Max missed them.

When your child is going through one of these more needy periods, try to separate from him as little as possible. You cannot force independence on a person, so don't make the mistake of "teaching" him to be independent by leaving him on his own. You'll only fuel his insecurities and make the neediness much stronger and longer-lived.

19.

Take the time you need for yourself.

Spending plenty of quality time with your child is crucial during the toddler years because so much development is taking place so rapidly. But unhappy parents can't raise happy toddlers. Recognize what you need to be the best parent you can be. Toddlers can be exhausting and parents need personal time to stay sane and happy. How much personal time depends on the parents.

If you take this advice as license to spend very little time with your toddler, you will probably have an unhappy toddler, and therefore not enjoy parenting as much as you could. Try to find just the right balance . . . enough personal time to keep you satisfied, and enough time with your child to keep your connection strong and loving.

20.

Don't sweat the tears.

Understand and know that your toddler will cry. Anything and everything that causes a toddler to feel sad, anxious, angry, frustrated or indignant can bring on a deluge of tears. Frequent crying does not necessarily indicate that a child is unhappy in the larger sense of the word. Crying several times a day is normal for a toddler because and he hasn't yet learned to put any restrictions on the expressions of his emotions. Aren't there several times each day when you feel frustrated or momentarily disappointed by something? You wouldn't dream of crying each time things don't go your way, but your child has not yet learned the coping skills you take for granted.

Nonetheless, your child's emotions are very real and sometimes scary to him. His crying should not be ignored, but you shouldn't over-indulge it either. If you consistently provide a calm, loving support system for him, he'll learn coping skills more quickly and easily than if you punish him for his emotional displays (ignoring is a form of punishing) or if you over-comfort so much that he decides he really must have something to be miserable about.

Do this exercise: Think for a moment about the last time you cried, really hard, all alone. Remember how you felt. Now think about the last time you cried, really hard, while someone you love held you and comforted you. How did you feel? Big difference, isn't there? Tears can be therapeutic, a release of stress and tension, and crying can make you ultimately feel much better, IF the crying is done in the presence of a loving, sympathetic companion. But without that presence, crying may actually heighten the level of tension and stress in a person.

If your child is angry with you he may well resist your attempts to hold him. Never force it. Just let him know that you are there for him when he's ready. You know your toddler best. If he cries much more than other children his age, or if he seems unhappy most of the time, talk with a professional.

21.

Set reasonable boundaries.

Your toddler is supposed to challenge you. It's her job. It's how she establishes her independence while discovering what the boundaries are in her world. You don't want to squash her will, but you do want to make those boundaries clear and un-confusing for her.

The enormous rate at which a toddler is learning and expanding her awareness excites her and causes her to operate on one speed only—full speed ahead! When you impose an obstacle or restriction, she is SUPPOSED to react as though you are treating her horribly unfairly. Her reaction does not make her spoiled or manipulative—it just makes her a toddler.

After she has come up against the same restriction many, many, many times, she will come to accept it. So don't expect to tell her once that the contents of your desk drawer are off limits. Unless you have the good sense to put a child-lock on the desk drawer, you will find her investigating its wonders on many more occasions, no matter how clear you make your wishes. She's not being bad; and she will eventually learn to bend to your desires, but at this age she simply can't resist testing those boundaries you impose upon her.

Shimm and Ballen say,

> Limits help give your toddler some balance in her difficult world. Without these boundaries a toddler can feel scared and confused about what she can and can't do. Although it can be upsetting to have your child angry at you when you say no, it helps her to figure out where her world stops and her parents' begins.
>
> Sometimes parents believe that their child will become more confident if they give him the freedom to make most of his choices. But this well-intentioned plan usually backfires. The parent who can rarely say no, who can't stand tears, and who says yes to virtually everything can make her child fearful of his power. If parents are afraid of having someone angry at them, and therefore a separate person, it becomes all the more difficult for a child to feel that he is his own person. He may have trouble saying no to anyone else because he has rarely heard his mother or father say the *N* word.

Do try to let your toddler make *some* of his choices and do things his way when you can. It will help his sense of self-esteem and make it easier for him to obey you on the other stuff. Make a list of the rules that are important and then ALWAYS enforce them. Any waffling will make it virtually impossible for him learn the rule. It will take a long time for him to learn it even when you are entirely consistent, and it is crucial that Mom and Dad (and all significant caregivers) present a unified front on all matters of discipline.

This may sound anal to some free-wheeling parents, but I believe you can't make up the rules as you go along. It's too hard to keep them straight, and too confusing for your little guy when they shift around. Sit down with your spouse and any other caregivers whose opinion you value and write down a set of guidelines.

If you're not going to allow food to leave the kitchen; if you're not going to allow jumping on or off the furniture; if you're not going to allow throwing of toys . . . then make those firm household rules. These are the kinds of issues that are easy to waffle on. It's not fair for your toddler to walk around the house with his cheese stick on Tuesday and be reprimanded for doing it on Thursday. It's tough enough for him to learn the rules when they're set in stone.

Make sure every caregiver has a written set of the rules, and has memorized them. Your toddler will become "well behaved" much more quickly this way. You will probably need to revise the list every few months as his skills develop and his activities change.

Penelope Leach writes,

Children need adults who have the courage of their convictions and the courage to set limits or draw boundaries for them, within which they know they can stay safe—and good. Limits are not just something adults impose on children. We all have to observe the limits that mark out our space from other people's—sometimes literally as well as figuratively. Children need additional limits, laid down by parents and caregivers, to keep them safe while they learn to keep themselves safe, to control them while they develop self-control and to make sure they don't lose their own space or trespass on other people's while they learn the lessons of socialized living like "do as you would be done by."

22.

Model, model, model!

None of us is perfect, yet we would like our kids to turn out that way. Take this opportunity to clean up your own act! You may never have such a great incentive again. Your toddler will copy everything you do. You are the basis on which he is creating himself. If you yell, he will yell. If you leave your belongings all over the house, he will not learn to put away his own belongings, no matter how much you nag him to do so. If you eat cookies, you can't very well deny him cookies. I finally defeated my life-long insatiable sweet tooth once I noticed that Tuck was enthusiastically showing interest in my less nutritive food choices. Once I stopped eating junk he lost (some of!) his interest as well and we're a much healthier family now.

In *The Discipline Book*, Dr. Sears reminds us, "The mind of a growing child is like a sponge, soaking up life's experiences; it's a video camera capturing everything a child hears and sees, storing these images in a mental vault for later retrieval. These stored images, especially those frequently repeated by significant persons in the child's life, become part of his personality—the child's self. So one of your jobs as a parent is to provide good material for your child to absorb." And Penelope Leach writes, " . . . your child will model his behavior on your example far more than he'll adapt it to what you say. In fact, if there's a credibility gap between what you say and what you do, he'll do what you do no matter what you say, so beware of old-fashioned disciplinary techniques like 'biting back' children who bite."

When we realize the tremendous impact we have on the way our children behave, we find the strength to make good changes in ourselves. Do you use bad language? Are you inconsiderate toward others? Do you want your child to behave in kindergarten the way you behave in your daily life?

23.

Attribute magic powers to "please" and "thank you."

Older toddlers are into magic. Use this developmental stage and the old cliché about "magic words" to your advantage. Here's what's magic about "please" and "thank you": They make grown-ups want to help you. Present them as such to your child. If you say that using these words is polite, expected, good manners, blah, blah, blah, your inducements are likely to fall on deaf ears. But if you're giving her license to practice magic, well, who could resist that?

"Please" will make her request more likely to be honored. (Be sure to explain that it's not fool-proof—it only *helps* her cause.) "Thank you" will make grown-ups happy and more likely to honor her future requests. And don't forget about "I'm sorry," so full of magic that it can fix hurts; and "Excuse me, please," which allows her to get the attention of distracted grownups.

The magic angle will get your child started, but the bottom line is that polite words and phrases will only become a part of your toddler's regular vocabulary if YOU use them consistently. Ultimately, she will imitate everything you do. Do things the way you want her to do them.

24.

Re-learn the meaning of PATIENCE.

"Patience" is a word that does not apply to toddlers. They don't have an ounce of it. They can't be comforted by promises of "tomorrow," because any time that is not RIGHT NOW does not exist for them. The concepts of "tomorrow," "next month," and "when you're eighteen" are all one and the same in toddlerworld.

For you, however, "patience" must become a mantra. One of the most beneficial things you can do to improve your relationship with your toddler is to build a generous cushion of extra time into everything you do together. Toddlers have a different pace. They find simple things amazing and worthy of lengthy inspection. If parents could tune into this mindset, they might really enjoy sharing

these experiences! But too often we're rushing from one place to another, possibly thinking we're doing it FOR the toddler, when in reality, he'd rather hang out on the sidewalk in front of the dry cleaner and spy on a grasshopper for twenty minutes.

Watch the grasshopper with him. Let him tell you his theories about grasshoppers. See if you can learn to enjoy getting lost in the present moment, and give your little Zen instructor a hug.

25.

Take toddler with you.

If your schedule permits, include toddler as much as possible in your daily life. Toddlers love being in new places and seeing new things as long as you keep them close and explain everything. Soon your errands and activities will be boring to your child. This is your last chance to spend lots of happy, quality time with her while accomplishing the things on your to-do list.

Keep a large bag stocked with interesting things to get her through the dull parts. I'm never without a revolving supply of small paperback books. They don't take up much room, they're light, and ounce-for-ounce they provide more entertainment value than toys. If you pull out the same tired book time after time, your child will lose interest (unless it's a favorite, in which case she'll want it read to her ten times a day from now until kindergarten). But if you stash a few new books in there every few weeks, you'll be ready for long cash register lines, doctor's office waits, and car rides (only when you're a passenger, please!).

Keep a few crayons and a little blank pad for impromptu creative expression. Fill small plastic containers with Cheerios or raisins. I sometimes sneak packs of party favors into my grocery cart. They're cheap and light and Tuck never fails to be delighted when later presented with a new plastic car, dinosaur, or sticker sheet while eating out or on some boring errand with me.

When you know you have a few hours or more of grown-up things to accomplish, make sure your little companion is well-fed and well-rested. Talk, talk, talk to her about every little thing you see along the way. You might want to plan mini-excursions to the park in between errands so that she gets a turn for some fun, too.

If your destination is a supermarket or one of those wonderful Target/K-Mart/Walmart type places, make a big deal about how cool and fun it is to ride in the cart. If you do this from the start, saying stuff like, "When we get to the store, YOU are going to get to ride in the CART!" you might be able to delay that day when your toddler insists that it's more fun to run down the aisles herself, grabbing everything she sees.

Of course, not all toddlers are created equal—or similarly. If yours hates shopping, don't bring her. Be creative in your shopping-avoidance techniques. Order groceries from markets that deliver to your door. Shop online and via catalog. With a little investigation, you may find you can all but eliminate the need to ever stand in line to pay for anything.

26.

Pretend you're as self-absorbed as he is.

Before your child gets into regular social interaction with his peers, begin introducing him to the rules of peaceful and respectful play. The next time you and he are playing, try treating him as if you were another toddler. Think about what that would mean.

When you build a block tower, does your toddler always gleefully knock it down? Most parents happily accept such behavior, but another toddler might not. Even if you feel silly insisting on this for yourself, teach him to ask you, "May I knock down your tower?" If you always say yes, he hasn't learned much, so occasionally you'll have to think as a toddler playmate would and tell him, "No, I'm not finished with it yet." Teach him that other people's creations deserve respect and admiration just like his do.

When you eat, do you let him sample your food in an unrestricted fashion? Many parents think nothing of allowing their toddlers to take bites out of their sandwiches or drinks from their cups. But a child who walks up to another child and takes a bite out of her sandwich may not be popular with his peers. And if you don't ever stop him from hitting you (even in fun) you can expect him to hit his playmates. He simply can't process the distinction. So at some point before his regular social debut, begin demonstrating the ins and outs of acceptable group behavior.

27.

Learn to appreciate your toddler's persistence.

Toddlers have a rep for being stubborn. Let's try rephrasing that and looking at it in a more positive light. A toddler with a strong will is a healthy, nicely-developing toddler. (Would you really want a *weak*-willed child?) When you say, "No, you cannot push your tricycle into the swimming pool," and he persists in trying every possible way to see that thing go down, he's showing a sense of determination that will serve him well in later years.

To him, a tricycle in the pool would be very exciting and no amount of logical explanation on your part is likely to dampen his desire. If you don't let him do it, how can he satisfy that burning need to learn? Would the tricycle float? Sink? Explode? He can't find out because you're in his way. I'm not suggesting you let him conduct his experiment. "No tricycles in the pool" or some variation on the theme likely exists in your code of conduct for him.

But instead of getting angry with his persistence, calmly intervene and talk to him about why he wants so badly to do it. Keep in mind, however, that unless your child is exceptionally verbal, an open-ended question like "Why do you want to do this?" is likely to get a blank look. Toddlers feel overwhelmed by questions that have an infinite number of possible answers. Instead, try to get into his head. Say, "I see that you really want to push your tricycle into the pool. Does it need a bath? Would you like me to help you wash it?" or "Did you want to go swimming today? Here, I'll show you the kinds of toys you can play with in the pool," or "Did you want to ride your tricycle? The pool isn't the right place for that. Let's see if we can name all the places that are good for riding a tricycle!"

If you can divert his attention without completely changing the subject, you may be able to lead him down a satisfactory path. But don't be surprised if your expert intervention still results in a meltdown. Such are the emotional upheavals of typical toddler life.

28.

Expect tantrums.

Tantrums are not misbehavior. They are an expression of your child's emotions. You may consider them an inappropriate expression, and that is fine. But realize that it will take time and patience on your part for you to teach your child more appropriate ways to express his negative feelings.

Tantrums are hard on parents, too, but do not punish your toddler for having them. He truly cannot help himself because he has not yet learned the internal controls necessary to monitor and contain his emotional responses to the many frustrations he encounters every day. Often the cause is an inability to communicate feelings, or anger at his own physical limitations or those you impose upon him. Sometimes it's just plain fatigue or a need to let off some steam. Anything that adds stress to your toddler's life—a new sibling or sitter or sleeping arrangement, for instance—will cause extra tantrums.

The best response to your child's tantrum is no response. As much as you feel your own stress level shooting into the stratosphere, try to stay calm, neutral and supportive. Do not become angry or you will surely worsen the situation. Don't become too doting either, or give in to a request you've just denied, or you will encourage more tantrums. Do stay close by, though, so your child won't feel abandoned on top of everything else. Shimm and Ballen say,

> It's important for parents to protect a toddler during her tantrums. If she
> destroys things or hurts herself she'll become even more frightened of her

strong emotions because her parents haven't been able to protect her from her rage. If your child starts to hurt herself you may have to hold her. But since this restraining action can escalate her anger, I'd recommend first removing all obstacles and then sitting quietly next to her . . .

Tantrums can really be horrible for a parent. However, if your toddler is having one because she's angry, scared, or frustrated, she may feel abandoned and convinced that her feelings aren't acceptable if she can drive you away. Try understanding that she isn't having a tantrum on purpose and needs you for comfort after the storm passes.

29.

Offer post-tantrum support.

After a child has finished with a tantrum, he is often in a mellow, relaxed mood—and very receptive to love and attention from you. Take this opportunity to reconnect with the child, even if the tantrum was directed at you. (Don't worry that you are enforcing the tantrum response and encouraging the child to have more tantrums. That would only be the case if your child did not get attention from you in other ways.)

Tell him that you understand angry feelings, or frustrated feelings, or sad feelings. Try to help him express the emotions that led to the tantrum. Tell him that those feelings are natural and everyone feels them sometimes. Then give him the opportunity to think about other ways he might have handled the feelings. You could provide suggestions. Say, "What if you had asked Daddy to help you with the dust-buster?" or "What if you had told me you didn't like the way I was combing your hair?" or "What if you had gone to your room and colored a mean picture?" or "What if you had jumped up and down until you didn't feel mad any more?" Shimm and Ballen suggest,

> Once your toddler calms down, explain in short sentences why he gets angry. "You really got mad when Mommy said it was time to put the crayons away. It's okay to be angry; next time you can tell me this. You can say, 'Mommy, I get mad when you tell me to put the crayons away.' Mommy will listen to you. And you

know I love you even when you are angry at me."

When parents articulate and label their toddler's feeling it helps a child to recognize and accept her emotions. You are teaching her how to communicate her feelings without resorting to tantrums . . .

After the tantrum has subsided and you are both feeling more in control, talk about how he can express himself with words. Think about how you can play act with him to get out his feelings. Use his toys and reenact a similar situation: "The mommy elephant gets the baby elephant really angry when she says no to more television."

30.

Judge the behavior, not the child.

Your toddler is not bad. Not even when he pees in your best pair of pumps on purpose. When teaching your child right from wrong, be sure to always separate the behavior from the child. He did a wrong thing, or a bad thing, but he himself is not bad. Never say, "bad boy!" but do let him know that certain actions are wrong and not permitted.

Now this is a tough one, but it is probably also wise to refrain from telling your child he is a "good boy." If he cheerfully puts all his toys away on Monday and you tell him he is a "very good boy" for doing it, what happens on Wednesday when he doesn't help clean up? Even if you don't say it, wouldn't he be likely to conclude that on Wednesday he is a "bad boy?" It is unrealistic to expect a child to behave perfectly all the time, so it is a mistake for you to tie his identity too closely to his behavior. He can be made to feel proud and happy about his good behavior and sorrow and regret about his bad behavior without making those behaviors the basis of his very person.

By all means, don't skip the praise, though! Parents do not praise their children nearly enough. When he puts his toys away, tell him, "I really like the way you're cleaning up! I feel so proud of you when you pick up your toys like that. You're making me feel happy!"

One of the biggest mistakes parents make is in responding more actively to misbehavior than to good behavior. Kids naturally crave attention—a big reaction from you is something they will strive for, whether the reaction is positive or negative. If you mostly ignore your child's good behavior, but become very focused on trying to correct the bad behavior, which do you think your child will be most likely to repeat? He is only looking for your attention. If you can shift your focus so that he wins the most attention from you when he does things right, you will soon see that his behavior shifts as well. That doesn't mean that you should ignore bad behavior. It just means you should correct it swiftly, calmly, and with as little fanfare as possible.

31.

Give directions effectively.

When you need to stop your toddler from doing something, or tell him to do something, or redirect the manner in which he is doing something, how you give the directions will have a big impact on the results you get.

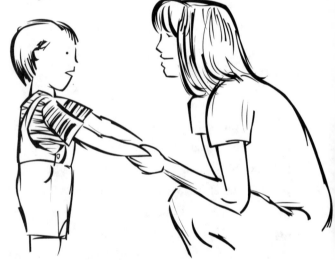

Way before your child can converse with you, he'll be able to understand much of what you say. But his attention span is still short, and easily diverted. Directions given from a distance have little chance of penetrating to any meaningful degree. And if you raise your voice a lot, the louder tone will soon have no effect.

The best way to get through to your toddler is to physically go to him, get down at his level, and look him in the eye. Say his name, then plainly say what he is to do. Say it confidently, as if you don't doubt for a minute that he will understand and do exactly as he is told. Don't say it in a threatening or angry manner or he may form a negative association to what you are saying. Even if it's something as benign and normally enjoyable as, "hold my hand," if you say it in an angry way a few times, he may suddenly think of hand-holding as a punishment and not want to do it.

32.

Encourage your budding artist.

Scribbling is the art of the toddler. She sees you using pencils and pens and wants to do the same. Early artistic endeavors will help your child learn to express her feelings. They're a precursor to more refined artistic ability and they provide another area for her to create and take pride in her accomplishments.

Give your child plenty of opportunities to let her creative juices flow, but be ready to supervise a little more closely since most art supplies are easy for toddlers to misuse. Some parents limit crayons, paints, chalk, and markers in order to avoid the discipline problem of kids writing on walls and furniture. Instead of limiting these valuable playthings, just take them out when you will be most involved in her play. If she's walking away from her paper with a crayon, ask her, "Are you done coloring? Let's put away that crayon then and find something else to play with." If she protests giving up the crayon, direct her back to the paper explaining that crayons are only for paper.

Here's a home-recipe for finger paints that are totally edible if not tasty: Mix two tablespoons of cornstarch into two tablespoons of cold water. Add one cup boiling water and stir. Use food coloring to color it. Put your child in old clothes (or none at all if the weather's warm and a bath can follow). Share the experience with her and show her how to combine colors for different effects. Give your own artistic urges a whirl.

Be on the lookout for art projects that can result from everyday activities. Save all your scrap paper in a special box, and pull it out when your child is bored. Show her how to cut designs with safety scissors. Glue scraps and leaves and odd "found objects" onto cardboard to create collage masterpieces. Encourage her to think beyond her eight-pack of crayons.

33.

Be understanding when you're on the phone.

Normally compliant toddlers will often whine and turn into daredevil acrobats as soon as Mom is happily chatting on the phone. I don't know what it is about the phone that seems to bring out the worst in a kid. I guess it's hard to see Mommy right there, physically accessible, but emotionally gone from reach.

One trick that almost always works for me and other nursing moms is to offer to nurse. The child feels connected and loved, he's nice and quiet, and you get to relax on the sofa for your phone chat. If you're not a toddler-nurser, try letting him have a turn talking. Say, "Aunt Aimee is on the phone! Would you like to talk to her? After you talk, here's a puzzle you can play with while I have a turn on the phone."

If that doesn't work, and he begs for your attention during your turn, don't just ignore him. He'll only try harder and harder until you

both are completely frustrated. Ask your sister to hold on, squat down to his level, and give him your complete attention for a moment. Maybe he just wants a glass of water. If you can meet his need quickly, do it, then tell him, "I'm going to talk on the phone, now. I'll be right here with you, but I want you to wait until I'm finished before you ask me for anything else, okay?" Sometimes this actually works. If you give him extra attention *after* every phone call, he might eventually condition himself to let you talk in peace.

34.

Don't yell!

Yelling is verbal and emotional abuse. It is scary and damaging to a child's self esteem. If his self-esteem is damaged, a child won't learn as easily, he won't behave well, and he won't be happy. If he's made to feel he's a bad person, he'll surely start to act like one.

If you're a frequent yeller, examine the effectiveness of this practice. Does screaming at your child really improve his behavior? Even if it occasionally scares him into compliance, have you taught him anything of value? If scaring him is necessary to control him, what will you do when he stops being frightened by your voice? The next logical step in a punitive punishment system would be to find another way to terrify your child into submission. Is that really the pattern you want to establish?

It's hard to break out of a rut, even one you recognize as destructive. But you can make a commitment to employ the morale-boosting discipline techniques in this book and others. The payoffs will be great not only for your child, but for you, too.

Besides, yelling can cause your child to become loud and unruly by sending a message contrary to the message you want to send. Lawrence Kutner points out that when a parent yells at a child to be quiet, "the message the child hears from the words stands in stark contrast to the more powerful message from the behavior. Clearly, the parent feels that speaking loudly is more effective than speaking quietly. The lesson taught is quite different from the lesson intended."

35.

Discipline with forethought.

Make your discipline routine routine. Know in advance how you want to react to different behaviors, and always make an effort to react the same way. It's easy to lose sight of this goal. One day your toddler throws his food on the floor. You're well rested and feeling happy and you tickle his feet while you're down there scooping up the mess.

The next day you're exhausted and late for a sure-to-be-grueling meeting. The sink is backed up, the phone is ringing and your toddler throws his food on the floor. You cry "NO! NO! NO!" while you rip the spoon out of his hand and scowl at him.

Your toddler now has no idea what to expect the next time he throws his food on the floor. Since it's his job to make sense of the world, he's obligated to repeat his experiment until it yields the same results often enough that he can move on to another experiment.

The best reaction would be a calm, boring reprimand that provides him no entertainment value or reason to repeat. Applied consistently, a response like that would probably curb the behavior.

36.

Set firm limits on television viewing.

Some childcare experts maintain that in the early years any TV is too much TV, but others take a more liberal position, believing that certain shows and videos can provide valuable learning experiences so long as their usage is not abused.

There are two big problems with toddlers in front of TV sets. The first is that TV viewing is such a passive activity that kids tend to "zone out" or mentally shut-down when they're doing it. Even if the subject matter is educational, the child's brain is on automatic, so he's not processing information in the same way that he is when he's actively involved in a more child-led learning situation.

The second problem is that the vast majority of what's on television is horrible for toddlers to watch. Violence is all over the place, even in much of what is termed "children's programming;" sexual and racial stereotypes are rampant; and most programs are just generally filled with examples of behavior that toddlers are better-off not emulating. Researchers have identified scads of negative effects on young children from watching irresponsibly-produced television shows.

A reasonable compromise seems to be to monitor very closely the content of your child's viewing as well as the time spent with the TV on. If your child has been creatively entertained all day and you need twenty minutes to send an important e-mail, you could probably pop a Sesame Street or Maisy tape in the VCR without too much guilt. And if you do a thorough investigation of the programs you allow your child to watch, you could broaden her horizons with your handpicked selections, especially if you watch them with her. Penelope Leach writes,

> The child who will not yet sit still for a book on natural history may watch a wildlife program and emerge with mental pictures of otherwise inconceivable wonders. The child who loves to be read to . . . may be able to hear good children's fiction read by the best narrators of the day. The city child can find out where the milk in those cartons came from; the country child can discover that there are other people and lifestyles in a world far bigger and more complex than she could otherwise know . . .
>
> If you offer only the few short programs you truly approve of, and that you or another adult will often share with her, your child will accept limited, highly selective viewing. If it has never occurred to her that the television set is a source of constantly dripping, easy entertainment, she will not bully you for more and more, at least not until she is old enough to read the program guides and play out sitcoms with other children in the school playground. And by then, hopefully her life will be too full of people and activity for television to take a disproportionate part.

37.

Utilize the magic of water-therapy.

On a real crank-demon day, take a bath with your little devil. Fill the tub extra full and take in some new bath toys that you find in your kitchen drawers. Play together, or lean back and relax while he entertains himself. A change of scenery often causes a change of attitude and baths provide an easy alternate setting when it's not convenient to actually leave home.

My friend Abby plops her bath-loving daughter into the tub whenever she needs to pay bills or make a phone call. Abby always stays in the bathroom with her, of course, but she says it's the only way she can be sure Jessica will stay happily entertained while Abby focuses on something else.

If the weather's nice, skip the bath and go for an outdoor swim. Fill up a little inflatable pool if you don't happen to have access to a real one. I've yet to meet a toddler who didn't love water-play. But never leave a young child in water alone, even if he was the star of his little-guppy swim class.

The American Academy of Pediatrics, by the way, does not recommend swimming lessons before the age of three. Though classes abound for younger children, those who take classes earlier are not any better swimmers in the long run. There is a danger that parents will mistakenly let their guards down, thinking their toddlers know how to swim when they really don't have the maturity yet to be safe around water.

Children under three who are submerged in water can be susceptible to water intoxication—meaning their blood can become overly diluted. So enjoy baths, kiddie-pools, and sprinklers, but don't set out to have the youngest swimmer on the block!

38.

Don't be a teeth-brushing drill sergeant.

Forcing a child to brush his teeth is kind of like forcing him to sleep or poop . . . it just can't be done. Sure, you could tie his hands together, sit on him, and pry his mouth open while you get in there, but is all that really preferable to a little plaque and tartar build-up?

Teeth-brushing just isn't worth waging major warfare over. Some (and I stress the word *some*) dentists maintain that before age three there is no real urgency to do thorough cleanings. It's best to get your child used to the idea of brushing his teeth well before then, but go at his pace. If you turn the whole procedure into a major ordeal, he might form lifelong negative associations to dental hygiene. (Yikes!)

Let your toddler watch you have a marvelous time brushing. Use the bubble-gum flavored toothpaste you bought for him so he won't think you're saving the good stuff for yourself. See if he'll copy you. If that doesn't work, offer to let him brush your teeth while you brush his. Ideally, you want him to practice doing a good job on his own teeth, but you want him to let you have a turn as well. (If you always brush his teeth for him, he'll never learn, but if you let him do it himself from the start, they're not likely to get too clean.)

Rely on any gimmick you can get

your hands on. Tuck absolutely loves the kid-friendly electric toothbrush we found for him. And a friend actually installed a fountain-like attachment to her bathroom sink which immediately caused her toddler to beg for tooth-brushings so he could rinse at the fountain.

As with any other habit you want to introduce, make it fun. Show him what's in is for him (he gets to be big like Mommy and Daddy; he gets to have strong teeth for biting his favorite foods; he gets his own special toothbrush to take care of . . .). Buy a spare toothbrush to keep as a toy and let him brush the teeth of all his dolls and stuffed animals. If you have a toothy alligator or shark, make it his special teeth-brushing buddy.

39.

Spare the rod . . . and the sarcasm and the frightening threats.

Slapping, spanking, bullying, ridiculing, forcing a child's hand, or instilling a sense of fear are all emotionally scarring forms of punishment. Some children will seek revenge. Some will become so self-loathing that they try to hurt themselves or hurt others. Some become afraid to do or try anything for fear of failure and ridicule.

There truly is no excuse to ever hurt a child. If you are doing anything that hurts your child, or feeling strong urges to hurt her, get yourself some help. No matter how deserving of a spanking you believe your toddler to be, realize that YOU are the one with a problem. Call the Parent Helpline of Parents Anonymous at 1-800-345-5044 for help in learning how to handle anger and discipline issues.

That said, adults are human, and may occasionally yell a little too loud or behave a little too threateningly. If you overreact to your child's misbehavior, apologize afterward and explain that you were wrong and you will not do it again. It's never too late. Don't be afraid your child will lose respect for you if you tell her you were wrong. The opposite is true. A child who sees you taking responsibility for your actions and working to correct them will be more likely to be responsible herself. You will be letting her know that mistakes can be corrected, and you will also be making it clear to her that it is never acceptable to hurt or demoralize another person.

These forms of vengeful punishment are not affective anyway, and they can make your discipline problems worse. Penelope Leach writes,

> Research shows that children who are physically punished are far more likely to remember the smack than what it was for, because they are often too angry to listen to explanations or crying too hard to hear them. Asked why they were smacked, four- and five-year olds usually say, "you were angry." So don't rely on physical punishments to teach your child good behavior. You cannot get the cooperation you need merely through using your superior physical strength.
>
> Be careful how you use your superior emotional strength, too. Punishments which are designed to make children feel silly or undignified are just as ineffective and emotionally dangerous as the physical kind. If you take away a child's shoes because he ran away, or force him to wear a baby's bib because he spills food down his clothes, you make him feel helpless, worthless, and quite incapable of learning the growing-up lessons you are trying to teach.

40.

Give reasons.

If you don't want your child to be a follower as an adolescent—one who is easily talked into taking drugs, drinking, or joining a gang—then don't use punishment tactics that enforce blind submission. Instead, make any request very rational and clear to your child, always pointing out why your suggestion is in his best interest. Don't say, "because I said so." Your child will never learn to think for himself.

Penelope Leach offers another good reason to avoid this phrase:

> Apart from emergencies, when reasons must wait until later, always tell your

child why he should (or shouldn't) behave in particular ways. You don't have to get into elaborate explanations for every little request, let alone into an argument, but if you insist that "because I say so," is all the reason he needs, he will not be able to fit this particular instruction into the general pattern of "how to behave" that he is building up in his mind. "Put that shovel back," you say crossly. Why? Because it is dangerous? Dirty? Breakable? Because you want to be sure of being able to find it next time? If you tell him that it belongs to the builders who don't like other people moving their things, he can apply that thought to other occasions. But if you say, "Just do as you're told," you teach him nothing.

Avoiding "because I said so" doesn't mean you have to give detailed *justifications* either. You don't need to convince your child of the rightness of your request. (Reasoning with toddlers is successful only in the most basic situations.) But you do owe her *some* explanation.

Say she wants to watch more TV than you feel is appropriate. You don't need to justify your position by launching into a whole big discussion about the difference between active and passive brain stimulation. Just say, "Because too much TV isn't good for you." True, it's not much more elaborate than "because I say so," but it shows concern for the child, and gives her a reason she can make sense of. Whether or not she agrees with the reason is not as important as the fact that you give one.

"Because (fill in the blank) isn't good for you," is a great blanket-statement reason for a lot of things that don't have other easy explanations. It helps a toddler feel safe by reminding her that you are an expert at taking care of her.

Watch your toddler for signs that something may be troubling her and offer reasons for anything she might not understand. She may be looking for answers without knowing how to ask the right questions. Shimm and Ballen write,

> Whatever is happening in your household should usually be reported to the toddler. Toddlers have inner antennae, and they believe they are the cause of everything from illness to grumpiness. It helps to explain and then reassure that most things in the family have nothing to do with them. For example, if the baby runs a fever and the parents haven't slept all night, now is the time to say: "Mommy and Daddy are feeling a little tired today because the baby is a little sick. No one makes anyone sick. You didn't make the baby sick."

41.

Honor your child's request to "Do it by self!"

At around two years old, many kids want to dress themselves, feed themselves, climb into their car-seats, wash their own hands and faces, and brush their own teeth. Some want to do only some of these things, and some are happy for you to do most of them until they are older.

Encouraging independence is most appropriate when you time your encouragement to coincide with your child's own instincts. Let him do "by self!" the things he wants, and occasionally suggest an activity you'd like him to do. When toys cover the floor, pull out the wagon and make a casual game out of the clean-up. Say, "Let's see if you can put all the toys that are on the floor into this wagon—all by yourself!" When he does, show him how to take the toys for a parade around the house, leaving each one off in it's designated spot.

The key to turning his blossoming independence to your advantage is to find a way to make him *want* to do the very things that you want him to do. If you try to make him do things simply because *you* want them done, it will just turn into a battle of wills. You're no match for him. It's rare for a grown-up to win in a battle of wills with a toddler.

Once this independence streak surfaces, do a thorough re-evaluation of your babyproofing. Most parents do a huge and complete babyproofing sweep right before baby starts crawling, and a year later they're still patting themselves on the back for all the money and time they spent. Remember that babyproofing a house is an evolving process. Toddlers develop new skills *fast* and many obstacles impervious to a 22-month old become gleefully challenging, but solvable puzzles to a 28-month old.

42.

Give in to requests that "Mommy do it!"

Sometimes toddlers want adults to do things for them (opposite of the "I do it by self!" syndrome) Your toddler may even switch back and forth between the two. When your toddler asks you to do something you'd rather she do for herself, give in. She's probably just recognizing that you can do it a lot better/faster/more neatly than she could, and she's trying to relieve herself of a little pressure or avert a frustrating situation.

Encourage her to help you or guide you as much as possible, so she can still take some of the credit. She may ask for your help with drawing a picture, putting on clothes even after she's learned to do it herself, or eating a particularly tricky food. Try showing her a simple way to do the thing, or try complimenting her on her skills more often so that she has more incentive to go at it alone.

43.

Ban guns.

"Boys will be boys." "It's an inborn part of their natures." "If you don't buy them guns, they'll just make their own from their Legos." I've heard all these comments from parents involved in the never-ending debate about whether or not to provide plastic weaponry for our children's entertainment.

My totally kind-hearted, generous and sweet husband has fond childhood memories of capturing and torturing little green army men in the name of patriotism; of hunting down his brothers and ambushing them with his life-size rifle, and warding off imaginary enemies with his BB gun. But he was a child during a time when real children didn't ever carry real guns; when fighting wars was a celebrated occupation for our country's young men; and when guns in the media were mostly used by honorable law-men protecting innocent citizens, not drug-kingpins, gang leaders and terrorists. Guns today are not what they were yesterday. Tragically, the concept of kids carrying and using powerful weaponry is no longer banished to the realm of make-believe.

While it is true that nearly all cultures since the beginning of time have observed violent play in their children (yes, particularly in their male children) observing it and encouraging it are two different things. I've read and heard that a boy pretending to shoot his playmate is not a cause of concern for parents and does not indicate a future career as a serial killer. I believe this to be true. But I still believe that it is irresponsible for toy manufacturers to provide realistic replicas of killing tools. After all, it is also natural for a toddler to hit a playmate, but we do not buy him brass knuckles to encourage more effective hitting.

Yes, I know that imaginative children will create the toys they wish to play with, and a gun can be easily fashioned from other toys or even by pointing a finger. But a child who uses his banana to pretend-shoot his sister one morning might use his banana the next morning to place a pretend phone call to his grandmother. A toy gun is forever a gun, and one sitting out in plain view will naturally inspire a child to pick it up and start shooting. Penelope Leach writes, "Research evidence strongly supports commonsense observation in suggesting that guns and weapons stimulate children to play more aggressively . . . " She also suggests,

> If you are thinking of banning weapons from your child's toy cabinet, do also review the place of other aggressive toys such as super-heroes. Groups of children who spend a structured play period with a layout of combat figures play more aggressively than children who spend the same period with farm animals or toy vehicles. Furthermore, during a subsequent period of free play, the children who have played with the combat toys continue to be markedly more aggressive than the others. A session listening to stories with aggressive themes . . . has similar effects, especially if children are encouraged to play the stories out. The same is true of older children who play violent video games in which players score more highly by killing more people, more horribly.

Aggressive play and violent play-themes may be universal, but it is clear that arming, peopling and modeling such play enormously increases its extent and intensity. So if you want to keep your child's play as nonviolent as possible, it is probably best to accept calmly games that come out of his imagination, realizing that at this stage, "Zap-bang you're dead" means no more and no less than "I'm it," but to make this one kind of play that you do not expand or facilitate. Do remember, though, that nothing you do or avoid doing about your children's toys and games will influence their orientation toward violence as much as what you do and avoid doing in your own behavior. All violence breeds violence, but real violence in the family, whether a child experiences or merely sees it, breeds more than play.

44.

Make grocery shopping an adventure in togetherness.

Let's face it, if the time your child spends with a sitter is limited (and whose isn't?) you're not going to relish wasting your precious Mommy-on-her-own hours in the grocery store. And you shouldn't have to, because if you allow enough time for it and schedule grocery shopping for your toddler's best peak performance times, it can be a fun adventure for the two of you to share.

Let him put the apples in the bag; open the crackers and let him sample; let him decide which vegetables you'll eat with dinner that night. Most importantly, TALK to him about what you're doing the whole time. Even a very young toddler will be entertained by your animated narration, and may understand more than you think.

My husband makes protein shakes every morning. Since he's the only one in the family who drinks milk, I would always tell Tucker as we got to the milk aisle, "Let's get the milk for Daddy's shake," and then I would let him pick out which particular jug we would put in the cart. One day when Tuck was just 22 months old, as I rushed past that aisle, he excitedly pointed and said, "Milk! Daddy! Shake!" I was grateful. I would have forgotten the milk that day.

Have a list made in advance of the trip. Show it to him, read it to him, and let him see you cross things off as the two of you accomplish them. Here's a time-saving trick: If you always get the same stuff, make a grand list and run off a bunch of copies. Then, before you go, adjust the list to that week's particular needs, perhaps crossing off the humus that wasn't eaten the week before, and adding once-in-a-while items like a birthday card for Uncle Mike or microwave popcorn for the movie you just rented.

Keep the marketing adventure funny for him. If he knows you're looking for bananas, pick up a bag of carrots and tell him, "Okay, I've got the bananas." Then, when he corrects you, say, "These aren't bananas? Are you sure? Oh, okay . . . " (putting carrots back) "Then where are those bananas?" (as you drive the cart slowly past the banana display, looking exaggeratedly in the other direction). When he "finds" the bananas for you, make a big show of how happy you are and how helpful he's being. (This only works if you're in the habit of being silly with your toddler. If you play it too straight, he'll just get confused about the names of his fruits and vegetables.) The thrill of correcting you and the challenge of watching you and checking that you're putting the right things in the cart will probably keep him mentally occupied and having a good time.

But again, no two toddlers are alike, and some toddlers just do not mix with grocery stores. If that's the case with yours, don't force the issue. Your time with your child should be spent—to the extent that's possible—in activities he enjoys, so try to use your solo-time for your marketing if you can't make it fun for him.

45.

Don't rush potty time!

Most children will give up diapers some time after their second birthday and before their third, but it could happen before two or any time in that third year, too. Signs of readiness include: dry diapers for two or more hours; interest in the potty and asking to sit on or use it; telling you when her diaper is wet or dirty, or better yet, telling you she needs to pee or poop. It will help the cause quite a bit if you let your child watch you when you use the bathroom. (I personally don't see how there's any other way, but I've heard of parents who somehow keep their bathroom habits private.) Without a model, a toddler may take longer to nail down the basics of toilet use.

When your child will be ready depends mostly on her personality, but also on a nearly impossible-to-detect internal development. She needs to be able to recognize the feeling of a full bladder and be able to control and release the flow of urine at will. She must also be able to recognize when she needs to have a bowel movement and be able to control the muscles so she can hold it until she gets to a potty. Some children gain this internal control at around two and many others don't gain it until three or even older.

Rushing your child to the potty before she's ready will only cause unnecessary frustration all around. Your toddler will feel bad about herself if she senses she's disappointing you. You will have to clean up lots of messes.

46.

Let him pick the pot.

If you think he's ready, take your child to pick out his own potty. Potty seats can either sit on the floor or up on the toilet. The advantage to the on-the-floor potty seat is that your child might feel more secure in a seat his own size, with his feet firmly planted on solid ground. The disadvantage is you'll have to clean out the removable little pot after every successful go-round.

The obvious advantage to placing the pot (or a ring) on your toilet is that you will be able to flush away your child's waste as easily as you flush your own (and he'd have to transition to the big pot eventually anyway). The disadvantage is that he'll have to climb up on a little stool (the stool is provided with the convertible seats) which he may love or hate and have varying degrees of success with.

If you don't already have a strong preference, discuss the options with your child. He may not be able to clearly tell you which type of seats he prefers, but as you describe them you may be able to discern by his reactions which one appeals to him most. Many of the seats available are convertible, which makes the most sense. You can start out with a floor-potty and graduate to a toilet-potty.

Let him try out the models on display. Most of the big baby stores will have a few seats to choose from. Make the shopping trip fun, but don't play up the excitement too much. You don't want to make toilet-learning a loaded issue.

Bring home the chosen potty and let your child help decide where it should go (unless you've already decided that the bathroom is the only place for such a thing). Some people leave the potty in the room where the child spends the most time. While it's still new and clean, let your toddler inspect its mysteries. Matter-of-factly answer his questions and explain what the different parts are for. Tell him that when he's ready he can use the potty, and when he starts to use it all the time he can wear big-kid underwear. He might want to sit on it, fully clothed, to watch a video or have a snack. Why not? The more comfortable he feels with the new piece of furniture, the more smoothly his transition will go.

47.

Figure out the best potty-teaching method for your family.

Are you one of those parents who can tell when your child is concentrating on pooping? Some kids get that faraway look, or stand perfectly still, or even hide or squat. If you can spot the signs, ask, "Do you feel your poopy coming?" (or "your BM" or whatever you call it at your house). Then ask, "Do you want to make your poopy in your new potty?" If the answer is affirmative, run with him to the potty. It's okay if the process has already begun, as long as there's something left for the potty, too. Wipe him yourself in the beginning, explaining how he'll do the wiping one day soon. Let him see his poopy in the potty. Let him flush it down if he enjoys flushing. It's never too soon to teach hand washing after every potty visit.

Some parents have told me that it helps to go buy training pants or even real underwear as soon as you get the potty. For some kids, the special grownup pants helps them get excited about the whole thing. If you take this daring route, try to bring the child to the potty about once every hour. Sit there with him, reading books together, singing songs, or just talking, so he doesn't get too fidgety.

Or, take the advice of family psychologist and syndicated columnist John Rosemond and leave the whole thing up to your toddler. He suggests presenting the potty, saying, "When you need to make poop or pee, use this potty the way grown-ups use the big potty. If you need any help, call me." He maintains that the more parents interfere, the more damage they can do to the process. If you think this style might work best for your child, try leaving him bottomless for a few days. He'll be able to feel those urges better that way, and it will be much easier for him to sit on the potty by himself and successfully complete the job. I'd keep a watchful eye out, though, so you can at least step in at the wiping stage. John Rosemond says,

> Parents should be role models and consultants to the child during this learning—available, but not hovering; helping, but not pushing. They should not, under any circumstances, follow the child around during the day, asking anxious questions like "Don't you think it's time you tried to use the potty?" When the child has an accident, as is inevitable, stay calm, reassuring, and supportive. Focus on success rather than failure, but keep praise low-key, lest you give the impression the child is performing for your benefit.

He also feels that most children are ready for the transition out of diapers between the ages of 24-30 months, and that missing the moment when a child is ready can be as problematic as rushing a child too early.

Here's another cute trick a friend used: Freeze colored water to make colorful ice cubes and toss a few in the potty before your child sits down. When the warm pee hits the ice, it will pop and make cool crackling noises as it melts. Fun to listen to and watch!

48.

Never punish for toilet-learning accidents.

If your toddler resists sitting on the seat, she may just not be ready. And even if she enthusiastically embraces the process, if she's having lots of accidents, it may be better to wait a few months and try again. Even if she is emotionally ready, she may not have the necessary internal control yet.

A child who feels too much pressure from loved ones will be too tense to control her bodily functions and therefore even more likely to have accidents. You can't force potty training. You have to let it happen. Don't get mad and don't try to bully your child. This is one of those battles you can't win, so don't let it turn into a battle. No matter what you do, you cannot force another person to pee or poop.

When she has an accident, calmly clean it up and put new clothes on her. Don't make her feel ashamed. Let her know that next time she can go in the potty.

49.

Demonstrate cause and effect.

Whenever possible, make a reward the natural result of the action that earned it. Doing so requires a little more thinking on your part, but it'll go a long way toward shaping your toddler's understanding of cause and effect. It will also make the reward feel less like a bribe.

Say you're having a hard time convincing your toddler to put her toys away when she's done with them. You could threaten her with a punishment: "Put your toys away right now or you're going into time-out." (Might work but nobody feels good.) Or you could appeal to her with a blatant bribe like, "If you pick up all your toys I'll buy you a new one when we go to the store." (Might work but she hasn't learned anything; or worse, she's learned that when she pleases you she deserves a material reward in return.) Try instead, "Pick up all your toys so that we'll have room to play Ring-Around-the-Rosie together on the floor here." Or even something like, "If you put away these toys quickly enough, we'll have time to read a story before dinner."

For younger toddlers, the reward will have to be immediately apparent, but at about two and a half, you can work with her on that difficult skill of delaying gratification. At his age, contracts start to work. "If you'll be cooperative for this shopping trip, we'll be done with it in time to stop at the park on the way home." Once she becomes comfortable with contracts, you can expect amazing negotiating skills to develop!

Of course, outright bribery does have its occasional place and has been a popular parenting trick for centuries. Penelope Leach says,

> Sometimes . . . material bribes—or, if you think they sound less immoral, prizes—can be very useful. Small children have a clear and simple sense of justice and are clear-sighted about other people's goodwill. If you have to make your child do something he very much dislikes, offering a prize may have the dual effect of making it seem worth his while to cooperate and making him realize that you are on his side. Suppose, for example, that it is a hot afternoon and he is enjoying himself in his wading pool. You have to pick up something for work tomorrow and you cannot leave him behind because there is nobody else in the house. What is wrong with a simple bribe honestly proposed? "I know you'd rather we stayed at home but we've got to do this errand. What about coming home by the store and seeing if your new video is in? Would that help?" It is a bribe but it is also a perfectly reasonable bargain.
>
> An actual prize sometimes makes all the difference to a child who has to put up with something genuinely unpleasant like stitches in his head. It doesn't much matter what the object is (as long as it isn't something he was expecting to be given anyway); what matters is having something nice dangling just the other side of the nasty few minutes. Don't make this kind of prize conditional on good behavior, though. A prize "if you don't make any fuss" may put your child under terrible strain. He may need to make a fuss. And he certainly needs to feel that you will support him however he behaves.

50.

Demonstrate responsibility.

As a corollary to your attempt to link a reward to the behavior that
earned it, try to find consequences that repair—rather than
repent for—a crime. If she angrily throws her bowl of
eggs on the floor, instead of scolding and sending her
to time-out, calmly say, "You've made a mess on the floor
with your eggs. Now you'll have to clean it up," while handing her
supplies. Of course you could do it quickly and more easily than she
could. And you'll probably have even more of a mess to clean up when she's
done with her attempt. But you'll be teaching her a valuable lesson.

She may have a wonderful time with her clean-up job, causing you to doubt that justice is being
served. But was it really necessary that she suffer? Isn't it better that she take responsibility to correct
her actions? After all, throwing that bowl on the floor was probably the result of frustrations that had
mounted to a level she just couldn't control. That doesn't mean it should be excused or ignored, but
perhaps she needn't be prosecuted to the fullest extent of the law.

51.

Help your child recognize joy.

A child's senses are more acute than ours are. Toddlers can experience unlimited joy from just singing,
jumping, touching soft things or squeezing clay. You can help and encourage your child to recognize
the joy in simple activities. Watch him and notice when he seems particularly delighted with
something. Ask him, "Do you like that? It looks like petting that kitten makes you really happy."

Encourage him to talk about being happy, and which things make him feel especially joyful. Sprinkle your activities with comments like, "Isn't this fun?" Even when he's feeling an emotion, it's good for him to label it so he can file it away and make it part of himself. The more he hears himself talking about his own happiness, the more he'll consider himself a happy person.

Help him *remember* happy things, too. After doing something nice together, talk about it. Say, "Wasn't that fun yesterday when we went swimming in the lake?" Bring up details and remind your child of all the parts you noticed him particularly enjoying. A friend of mine asks, "What was the best thing that happened today?" as a part of her toddler's bedtime ritual. Talking about and remembering that "best thing" makes for pleasant drifting-off-to-sleep thoughts. It also gives her great insight into her toddler's world.

52.

Plant the seeds of empathy.

Toddlers are not naturally empathetic creatures. They sincerely believe that every person, animal and object they come into contact with is here for the express purpose of benefiting them in some way. Other toddlers are enjoyed and tolerated only as long as they obey and entertain. When a conflict arises, a toddler is very far from being able to see it in any kind of objective light. All objects are MINE in toddler world.

But that doesn't mean you, the parent, shouldn't go out of your way to start planting the seeds of empathy. When your sweetie grabs the fire truck out of the hands of her playmate, say, "When you take a toy away from Nicholas, he feels sad. Do you remember when Sara took your giraffe away? Do you remember how sad it made you feel? Please give the fire truck back so he won't feel sad." Likewise, if hitting or biting is a problem, you may get better results from saying, "When you bite Cindi, it hurts her, so don't do it again," than if you just snapped, "No biting!" It will take many such conversations for your message to sink in, but don't give up. Eventually, when you least expect it, your empathetic little angel will parrot back your words.

Let your child witness your empathetic behavior toward others. And above all, empathize with her. Nothing eases a toddler's frustration better than an understanding parent giving voice to her concerns when she herself is unable to articulate them. Shimm and Ballen point out,

> Just think how validated and empowered adults can feel when someone reports in a nonjudgmental way on their mood. "Boy, you really have had a lousy day. It must have been hard when your toddler had six tantrums at your mother-in-law's house." So imagine the relief that a toddler with a limited vocabulary and understanding of her emotions can feel when someone describes in simple words what she is doing and feeling. Parents help their toddler separate by distinguishing her feelings from theirs and others'.

Another super technique for empathizing with your older toddler is to say, "When I was your age, I felt the same way." This kind of understanding helps a child cope with all kinds of fears, jealousy, angry thoughts, and self-doubts. It lets her know that nothing is wrong with her for feeling the way she does, and gives her hope that the feelings will get better as she grows. (You don't have to actually remember feeling the emotion to give your child this kind of support. Just trust that whatever she's feeling is probably normal and you probably did feel it at one time or another, too.)

53.

Make up songs and games.

Cutting those itsy bitsy nails . . . trying to change a wiggling, flopping toddler's diaper . . . rinsing shampoo off a loudly protesting little head . . . these universally common parenting pitfalls make even the savviest mommies and daddies groan. Toddlers don't like being told what to do, especially when it involves being passive and still.

But every toddler-grooming task does not have to become a battlefield. All a creative parent has to do is figure out a way to turn the dreaded deed into a fun event. Think along the lines of: What's in it for her? It takes some effort initially, but once you've established a new pattern you can reap the benefits forever (or at least until she starts trimming those cursed nails herself). The following two ways demonstrate examples of turning favorite songs into games that can facilitate problem tasks. Make up your own to suit your needs. Songs and games can ease the trauma of hair-washing, nose-blowing, teeth-brushing, and more.

54.

Sing and smooch your way to happier nail-clipping times.

Trimming your toddler's nails MIGHT actually become fun. Try singing the "Where is Thumbkin?" song with these revised lyrics (if you don't know that song, sing the following words to the tune of "Frere Jacques"). Let her practice producing each finger by name. Then pretend your nail clippers are a sweet little bunny or other animal and introduce the imaginary Clipper bunny to your toddler.

Tell her that Clipper wants to kiss her fingers and when he does, his little teeth will trim her nails. Let her make a fist and hide her fingers until each one is called out individually to play the kissing game. When it is Mommy's turn, kiss each finger as the song suggests. When it's time for Clipper to kiss each finger, sing, "Clip, clip, clip," as you trim that nail. (If anyone other than Mommy is clipping, substitute the correct name!)

Where is Thumbkin? Where is Thumbkin?

Here I am! Here I am!

Mommy kisses Thumbkin! Clipper kisses Thumbkin!

SMOOCH! SMOOCH! SMOOCH!

CLIP! CLIP! CLIP!

Where is Pointer? Where is Pointer?

Here I am! Here I am!

Mommy kisses Pointer! Clipper kisses Pointer!

SMOOCH! SMOOCH! SMOOCH!

CLIP! CLIP! CLIP!

Where is Tall Girl? Where is Tall Girl?

Here I am! Here I am!

Mommy kisses Tall Girl! Clipper kisses Tall Girl!

SMOOCH! SMOOCH! SMOOCH!

CLIP! CLIP! CLIP!

Where is Ring Man? Where is Ring Man?

Here I am! Here I am!

Mommy kisses Ring Man! Clipper kisses Ring Man!

SMOOCH! SMOOCH! SMOOCH!

CLIP! CLIP! CLIP!

Where is Pinky? Where is Pinky?

Here I am! Here I am!

Mommy kisses Pinky! Clipper kisses Pinky!

SMOOCH! SMOOCH! SMOOCH!

CLIP! CLIP! CLIP!

55.

Occupy the wiggle-worm while you change that diaper.

Does your sometimes too-energetic toddler do the wiggle dance on the changing table? Maybe diaper changes don't have to be so hard! Try acting out the following movements while you sing these words to the tune of "Twinkle, Twinkle, Little Star." Show him how to do the hand movements. Repeat the "keep still" verses as long as you need to finish the change, or invent other ones (touch your eyes, chin, shoulders, etc.). Wiggle the child's whole body before and after the change, as the song suggests. Concentrating on the hand movements will keep him distracted from trying to roll or kick, and also keep those little hands up and out of your way!

Wiggle, wiggle, little friend.
Dance and shake your bottom end.
Can you wiggle just your nose?
Can you wiggle just your toes?
Now, keep still, keep still, little friend.
Keep so still your bottom end!
Wave your hands up in the air.
Touch your ears and touch your hair.
Keep still, keep still, little friend.
Keep so still your bottom end!
Can your fingers touch your head?
Can they touch your cheeks instead?
Keep still, keep still, little friend.
Keep so still your bottom end!
Hear your hands go clap, clap, clap!

Hear your clothes go snap, snap, snap!
Now wiggle, wiggle, little friend.
Dance and shake your bottom end!

I do a variation on this song whenever I have to take Tucker into a public restroom with me. To keep him from touching anything, I sing about him touching his hair, ears, shoulders, elbows, etc., the whole time he has to stand there waiting for me.

56.

Distract!

Even though your toddler is a lot savvier than the baby he used to be, you can still use clever distractions to head off trouble. Say he's getting restless waiting for company to arrive for a holiday feast at your house. He's decided he wants to fingerpaint—an activity that requires old clothes, your close supervision, and a tolerance for mess. He's about to get very insistent and your flat denial of his request will surely result in a meltdown. An option would be to quickly pull out your best distraction techniques.

He might forget about fingerpainting if you started jumping up and down, screeching and scratching your armpits like a monkey. Say, "I'm a tickle-monkey and I'm gonna get you," as you chase him around the house. Of course you'll probably have to chase him, catch him, tickle him to the ground, and continue being a monkey or some other fascinating creature until your guests arrive. But you'll have saved yourself a tantrum and gotten the little host of the house in a good mood for a party.

Being of a somewhat naturally silly nature, I use pretend-games as distractions all the time. They work to diffuse a wide array of unpleasant situations. He wants cookies at the grocery store. I'm suddenly hard-of-hearing. "You want *what*? Wookies? What's wookies? Oh, *nuggies*? You want nuggies? Okay, here are some nuggies on your head." By the time we've stopped nuggie-ing one another and laughing, we're a few safe aisles away from those trouble-making cookies.

Make silly faces. Pretend you don't know how to do something and do it wrong while asking your toddler for help. Tuck thinks it's hilarious when I forget where socks go and accidentally wear them on my ears, or I forget how to set the table and all the plates and cups are upside down. Become Elmo by using his voice and expressions (or Barney, if that's who floats your child's boat). A toddler who won't take a bath for Mommy just might agree if it's at Elmo's request. You can also become a favorite animal, or hold up a stuffed animal or doll in front of your face and talk in an altered voice.

When your toddler gets antsy in the car, try making some weird, unexpected noise. Sing his favorite song in a silly operetta way, or sing the alphabet song with the letters all jumbled (he'll only think that's funny if he knows the alphabet). Use your buttons to raise and lower his window. Hold one of his dolls by the hands as you hold the steering wheel and tell him Woody (or whoever) is driving the car.

57.

Give up control (sometimes).

Control is at the heart of almost every toddler-parent clash. While it is right and natural for a growing child to gain more and more control over her circumstances as she grows, for some toddlers, control is like a drug. Once they get a little taste of it they'll do anything for more, more, more! These toddlers may suddenly refuse to eat, sit in a car seat, wear any parent-selected clothing, or do anything they are asked to do.

If this sounds familiar, consider the possibility that you are trying to control too much. Toddlers sometimes become obsessed with control when they are not given enough of it. While all children need firm limits in order to thrive, they also need to have their desires respected and sometimes granted. Of course, giving a toddler too much control will cause problems as well. The trick seems to be in avoiding direct battles. Give her control of some of the details, while retaining your authority as director of the show. Shimm and Ballen say, "He acts out of bounds not because he is purposely out to drive you crazy, but to establish his independence. Therefore, be a benevolent dictator; when you set rules, remember to give him his share of power."

According to Dr. Sears, parents who try to exert too much control over their toddlers tend to think of them as manipulators out to dominate the parents. He says,

> This sets up an adversarial relationship between parent child, and confuses taking charge with controlling the child. Authoritarianism creates a distance between the parent and child for two reasons: It is based on punishment, which can easily create anger, and thus distance the child from the parent, and it makes little or no allowance for the temperament or developmental level of the child. Wise disciplinarians become students of their children and work to know their children well. Controllers often find this consideration demeaning to their authority and therefore do not believe it belongs in their discipline package. Because authoritarian parenting is not geared to the child as an individual, this style of parenting seldom brings out the best in parents and child, even when a warm heart is behind the heavy hand.

58.

Prepare for that first professional haircut.

To expect a toddler to sit still and be pleasant during a first (or second or third) professional haircut is an unrealistic expectation. Try to prepare him in advance. Read books about going to get a haircut. Cut a little piece of your own hair and show him that it didn't hurt you. Explain how hair grows back, complete with photos of him from a bald baby to a long-locked toddler. Make a fun game out of playing pretend haircut. Let him sit in a chair while you use your fingers as imaginary scissors all over his head. Then you be the victim while he's the haircutter. If you think he'll sit still for it, take him to watch you or your husband get a haircut. Chat pleasantly with the hairdresser to display to your toddler what a nice time you're having.

When the big day arrives, go to one of those kid-friendly places if you can. Some have toys, VCRs playing videos, and a bubble-blowing staff. Getting your hair shampooed by leaning back in those big seats can be scary stuff so wash his hair before you go, and ask the stylist to just spritz it with some water before cutting it.

Hold him in your lap if he's freaking out. Some kids respond better when they can see what's going on in the mirror; others are scared by seeing the procedure, and should be turned away from the mirror. Be understanding and don't feel embarrassed if he's terrified. The people who work in these salons have seen it all before. Don't minimize his fears, but don't make too big a deal of them either. If you become stressed out by his protestations, he'll register that you're scared too and that will reinforce his fear. Try to keep a smile on your face and chat happily with the stylist until the job is done. Then congratulate him on having gotten through it and tell him you know he'll be less scared the next time.

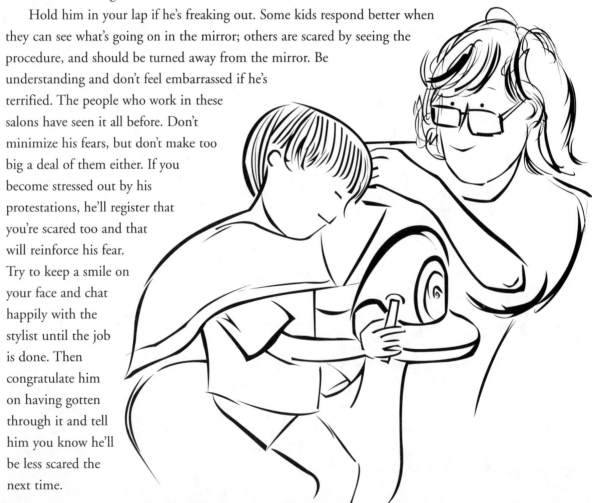

59.

Learn coping skills for the Destruction Zone.

Kids wreck stuff. Toddlers are notorious book rippers, glass breakers, graffiti artists, and toilet dunkers. Their motives aren't (always) malicious, though. Often, what appears to be a destructive act started out as a simple science experiment on the part of the toddler. "I wonder what will happen if I throw this cordless phone against the wall . . . "

Even after you state a rule, this whole business of throwing gets tricky for the toddler mind. Why is it okay to throw soft toys and balls (and maybe even pillows if you live in a really fun house) but not okay to throw harder stuff? How can you really define "harder stuff" for a toddler anyway? And if you allow gentle throwing that's low to the ground, where do you draw the line on defining throwing that's too high and a danger to people and belongings? Recognize that your rules, while clear-cut to you, might at times be too subtle for your child to fully grasp. Be understanding and instructive with your corrections, and he'll start to see the big picture more clearly.

When you sense that an honest educational experiment is being conducted, correct the behavior gently, explaining your cause. But destruction that is deliberate will require different handling. Sometimes a child will deliberately do damage in order to release pent-up frustration over not being able to master a skill or being stopped from doing something he wants to do. If that's the case, a time-out will help him learn to control his destructive impulses. At a calm moment, guide him through some better stress-release techniques.

Of course, there's always the chance the child is acting out to get your attention. If you think that may be the case, be sure to shower him with plenty of happy attention while he's being good, and try to minimize your reactions to his negative behavior. Remember, any reaction is a welcome reaction to a child whose main concern is to get your attention.

60.

Make mealtimes peaceful (sort of).

A happy toddler is a toddler who is not expected to perform social niceties that are beyond his natural developmental ability. Don't insist your child sit through long meals in a high chair or booster seat if he has repeatedly demonstrated how much he hates it. It's okay for him to kneel in a sturdy chair that's made for grownup people if that's what he wants to do. It's okay if he gets up and runs around during mealtime, as long as he returns periodically to actually eat. Some families have great success with a child-sized table and chair next to the adults' table. This allows the toddler to come and go freely, and often results in the child eating more in the long run.

Battles over food consumption are common between willful toddlers and worried parents. But if you can bring yourself to leave your child alone, he really will get what he needs. Your job is merely to provide the *opportunity* for him to eat a variety of healthful foods. Sometimes a toddler will get on a carbohydrate jag, or want nothing but burgers for a solid week. Indulge it as much as you can. According to the American Academy of Pediatrics, a toddler is meeting his nutritional needs if he manages to eat something from each food group every two or three days.

Dr. Sears says,

> Don't use food as a control tool. Never push food on babies or children. If they want it, they'll either open wide or pick it up themselves. It's your job

to provide healthy nutritious food. It's your child's job to eat it. Never chase your child with a spoonful of anything. Never use the threat of "no desert" to get a child to finish his main course. ("If you don't eat your peas, you can't have pie.") Don't even talk about how well or poorly a child has eaten. Zip your lip. It's his stomach."

If you're really freaked about your child's consumption, loosen your restrictions on how and where food is to be enjoyed. He might want to eat, but not enough to sit at the table for it. When Tuck is completely uninterested in having dinner with us, I sometimes sit on the floor with him and we play with his toys while he eats. He eats a lot more that way; he's a lot happier, and I believe there's plenty of time to change the pattern once he's older and will be better able to sit still for mealtimes.

61.

Stay cool in the face of embarrassing comments.

"What a fat man!" "That lady is old." "Why is that guy brown?" Toddlers say it like they see it. If the person under your child's scrutiny is within earshot, keep your answer quick and simple. Say, "People come in all kinds of shapes, colors and sizes, and being different from one another is part of what makes us all special."

Then QUICKLY change the subject to the most fascinating topic you can think of to keep her from worsening the situation with more questions or observations. If you're able to communicate with her privately, give the above explanation, but also add that saying that someone is fat could make that person feel bad so she needs to learn to speak more quietly when she's telling you about people she sees.

Don't overreact and shame your child for an honest observation just because she has inadvertently embarrassed you. Since she is used to sharing her observations with you—and since you probably applaud them for the most part—make sure she knows that she can always talk to you about the things she notices in other people, but it's better if she will do so in a soft voice so that only you can hear her.

Read books about people of other cultures and about handicapped people—and when your toddler is old enough to appreciate them, about anyone who doesn't fit in. Your goal is not for her to stop noticing differences, but to accept them freely and without intolerance. If the adults she spends the most time with harbor no prejudices, it is unlikely she will form any of her own.

62.

Take whine-prevention steps.

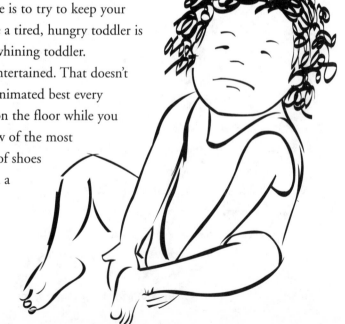

Man, I hate whining. Give me a full-blown outburst any day over a nagging, insistent whine. Luckily, whining doesn't have to become a regular in your toddler's arsenal. Your first line of defense is to try to keep your child reasonably well-rested and well-fed since a tired, hungry toddler is usually just a few toddles away from being a whining toddler.

Next, try to keep her at least somewhat entertained. That doesn't mean you have to be at her side and at your animated best every moment. But if you plan to leave her sitting on the floor while you balance your checkbook, at least pull out a few of the most interesting toys in the toy box, or a few pairs of shoes from your closet, or something she hasn't seen a million times before, for her to play with.

When Tucker started whining I was completely honest with him about it, even though I thought he was too young to really understand. I told him, "When you talk that way, it makes my head hurt. When my head hurts, I will want to say 'no' to whatever you are asking me. If you ask in your regular voice, I will want to say 'yes.'" He needed reminding every so often, but he really did catch on and whine less.

Most importantly, listen to your toddler when she tries to communicate with you. A lot of whining is just the result of a child's frustration at not being heard. Your whine-prevention plan will never be fool-proof however, because, once again, toddlers just insist on being toddlers.

63.

Don't whine back.

It's amazing how often you hear a parent whine to a child, "Will you PLEASE stop that whining?" Pleading with a child to stop whining doesn't work because toddlers don't have a clue what you're talking about. Plus, by using the same annoying tone of voice you're trying to correct you're just confusing the issue further. Instead, determine your intent as quickly as possible. If she's whining for you to play a video for her, and if you have promised to play the video and fully intend to do it as soon as you finish folding the laundry, drop that sock and pop in that video at the very first hint of a whine. Otherwise, if you keep putting it off, you will be rewarding the extended whining later when you eventually give in.

If, on the other hand, the whining is about something that you have already said "no" to, don't give in under any circumstances. Whining needs correcting as much as tantruming, so use the same rule of thumb: once a NO, always a NO. Never reward behavior you want to curtail. To do this sometimes takes a will of steel and you must be prepared to summon up every ounce of fortitude. There will likely be times when you want the whining to stop so badly that you'd do anything to restore peace. Don't give in! Even if you suspect you made a poor call, and the answer should have been yes, save that yes for the next time she asks. For this round, you are committed.

My friend Carol reports success with the temporary deafness technique. While her toddler is whining, Carol says, "Hmmm . . . I can't hear what you're saying when you say it that way. I can only hear you when you talk in your nice voice." If consistently applied, and if the child isn't too upset, this can work to reduce the recurrence of whining. But if the child is very sensitive or genuinely distraught, it can backfire.

If you use this technique, and if the child then repeats her request in her sweetest voice, you may want to go ahead and give her what she wants if it's not a big deal to you (and if doing so doesn't reverse an already-established "no"). If you can't give her what she wants, you will have to take extra care in explaining that you love the way she asked and you are proud of her for using that voice, but unfortunately, the request is still denied. Try to come up with some compromise that satisfies both parties so she will still be encouraged to ask for things in the way you'd like.

Dr. Sears offers the following additional tips:

> Keep on talking and distract the whining child into other interests: "Oh, look at this pretty flower. Let's see what it smells like." You're letting the child know that whining doesn't bother you.
>
> If whining persists, replay for your child how unpleasant it sounds, being careful not to mock. Don't do this when you are both emotional. Do it at a calm time . . . "Which do like, Mommy's sour voice ('I don't wanna make supper') or Mommy's sweet voice ('Gosh, I'm tired. I could use some help')? Once your child learns that whining doesn't work (and her language skills improve), whining will be a sound of the past.

64.

Understand your toddler's anger.

Anger is normal. Everyone feels it, and since toddlers are us without our restraint systems in place, they are likely to display their anger in a big way. Let your little protester know that it is okay to feel angry and okay to express his angry feelings.

But if his angry outburst includes any form of assault on other people or destruction to property, make it clear that those actions are unacceptable to you. Help him use words to express what he is feeling. Most of all, don't get angry back. It will only fuel his fire and prolong the unhappiness for both of you.

Dr. Sears says,

> Don't let your child stuff anger. Encourage your child to recognize when he is angry, starting when he is a toddler. Be an attentive listener, helping your child talk about feelings. Given a willing audience that shows empathy rather than judgment, children will often talk themselves out of their snits.

65.

Stay sane while indulging your toddler's imagination.

"Mommy, you the doggie. Me the kitty cat."

So you crawl around, bark, howl, roll over—and for you, that about wraps up the game. Not so for your child—excuse me, *kitty cat*—who could continue licking and purring for forty-five minutes, fully expecting you to stay in your role as well. Most parents recognize the importance of imaginative play in fostering their children's creativity and intellect, but some grown-ups have a hard time joining in.

Push yourself to get over that initial hump. You've decided you're going to spend this time playing with your child, so enjoy it! See if you can really immerse yourself in the playing. You can't have fun if your efforts are only halfhearted and your mind is on the office.

If you're tired of being the doggie, tell her that the doggie turned into a lion. She won't mind as long as you are still as involved in the game. Or use the game to accomplish something you needed to do anyway. Doggies and kitty cats have to eat, so whip up some pet-chow (last night's leftovers chopped up in a bowl) and have lunch in character. Maybe the doggie and kitty have fleas and need to take a flea bath. As long as you keep the pretend part lively, your child will likely cooperate. I can't tell you how many afternoons I've spent as Elmo, the Easter Bunny, or Maisy's friend, Telulah.

You can have fun with other kinds of imaginary play, too. Make up skits with those little plastic people. Show her how to make them walk around, hug each other, jump, etc. Make up conversations between them, and soon she'll be doing the same. Amuse yourself, or use the principles of play therapy to work out your own stress. Even if the humor goes over your toddler's head, she'll have more fun if she senses you're having fun. And watching you exercise your imagination is the best jump-start for her own imaginative games. The more you indulge in this kind of play with her, the sooner she'll be happy playing by herself.

66.

Take turns.

If she wants to play the same game over and over, or if the game she plays really bores you, give her a little lesson in taking turns. Set a timer and tell her that you'll play her game for ten minutes more, and then Mommy picks the game. Be sure she is included in your game, and try to make it fun for her, even if your game is "Let's unload the dishwasher!"

Be fair with the timer, and let her choose the next game. And be on the lookout for activities you both enjoy so that she won't dread letting you have your turn. There are some cute exercise videos for toddlers (Elmocize is one of our favorites), and a creative Mommy can turn them into a good workout for herself, too. You'll have more success in making exercise a shared, fun experience if you choose a tape for kids than one for adults. Tuck and I love practicing our yoga together with his Yoga Kids video (available through Living Arts, 1-800-254-8464.)

67.

Give warnings before switching activities.

Toddlers need time to adjust to any transition. If the doctor is in the middle of surgery on his favorite bunny rabbit he's going to resist being told to come to the table "right this second" for dinner. But if he has a five-minute warning, he might be able to wrap up that appendectomy and leave the patient to nap while he scarfs down a few fish sticks. You could ease the transition even further by inviting the patient to come to dinner as well. Some macaroni and cheese might speed his recovery.

Remember that your toddler can't tell time yet. He has a vague feeling that it seems about dinner time, or tooth-brushing time, or bedtime, but he still needs you to blow the start whistle. Imagine how you'd feel if you were involved in an activity you enjoy and someone told you "It's time to go to the grocery store. Now! Get up, get in your car, go!" As adults, we have some control over the pacing of our lives. If you give your child warnings that events are going to occur, he'll feel less imposed upon by your requests, and be less likely to resist them.

It's particularly hard for some toddlers to leave the homes of other children. I secretly suspect that the new and exciting toys at the host's house are at least as alluring as the actual playmate. If you're leaving a friend's home and your child is very involved in the dollhouse there, say, "It looks like you're having fun with that house. You can play with it for five more minutes and then we will get in the car to go home." Then, when the minutes are up, get down on the floor, look him in the eye, and say, "It's time for us to go home now. Say bye-bye to the nice house."

Of course, there will be times when warnings are impossible, or your child resists anyway. See if you can bridge the transition with some carry-over suggestion. "We have to go pick up your sister now, but why don't you bring Pooh and Piglet along? They can finish sharing that honey in the car," or "I bet Maisy would love to watch you brush your teeth."

68.

Keep talking.

Remember that your toddler's understanding far exceeds her ability to make herself understood. Real language usually starts kicking in around the second birthday. It's a really fun stage because if you spend enough time with your toddler you'll learn her language well enough to truly have two-way conversations in ways you never previously could. It is so cool when you start to figure out what her associations are. Listen! What seems like random garbledygook is often actually following some logical progression.

Babies learn to talk by listening to you talk. You probably said a lot of things to your baby that you didn't think she understood for a long time before she started parroting back to you. Sometimes it's tempting, when your toddler starts conversing in earnest, to do your own version of parroting. You're so anxious to communicate with her that you adopt her language. While doing this is normal, and kind of fun, remember that it does nothing to further your child's skills.

First of all, you don't need to talk like her for her to understand you. She's been understanding you for a while now, or she wouldn't be mastering speech as well as she is. Secondly, it's the challenge of learning new words that's fueled her progress thus far. You'll need to be clear and concise when her understanding is most important, as in issues of discipline, but you can also increase, by tiny increments, the vocabulary you use with her.

Make your observations ever-more detailed and specific, always speaking at a level just above the level you believe she understands. You'll be amazed at how quickly her comprehension will grow. Label things by size, shape, and color, as a regular part of your conversation. Ask her lots of questions, and don't ever be disappointed by her answers. They'll get more accurate and more detailed with time.

And don't be concerned when your toddler goes through a talking-to-herself phase. She's not crazy. She probably can't easily distinguish between thinking and talking. Pay attention, and you'll get a cool glimpse into how her mind works. We all actually talk to ourselves, but grownups are used to doing it silently. Toddlers don't worry that people will think they're crazy. They're just doing what comes naturally.

69.

Praise and encourage, but not too much.

There's a lot of controversy over the issue of parental praise. Some experts say kids actually should not be praised for their achievements—that it's healthiest for them to feel satisfaction within themselves for a job well done. Others say that a parent should praise only in the exact measure that a child seems to be proud of himself. Some say parents should heap on the praise in order to elevate a child's confidence, but then others warn that a child won't learn how to objectively judge his own accomplishments if too much praise is given. They worry that telling a child he's the "best" at something sets him up for competitive feelings later, and creates a perfectionist who isn't happy unless he's truly the best at what he's doing—meaning better than anyone else he knows doing it.

Perhaps a middle ground in all this conflicting advice would be to praise children frequently, but ONLY to the extent that the praise is genuine. If the child is attempting to draw a horse and his picture looks absolutely nothing like a horse, you could still say "I love the colors you used in this picture!" If he's trying to pull his shirt over his head and can't quite manage it this time, I think it's okay to say, "You did a great job taking off your pants and your socks, and a great job trying to take off that shirt."

If he usually can take the shirt off, you could add, "I know you can pull your shirt off, too, when you're not so tired."

Watch your child for clues. If he seems uncomfortable with the level of praise you're dishing, cut back. You don't want him to come to mistrust your judgement of him. On the other hand, if he seems always to be desperately seeking approval from you, perhaps you need to up the dosage you've been administering.

Always praise the action, not the person. The more specific your praise, the more meaningful it will be to him and the more he'll want to repeat his commendable behavior. Tell him, "I love how you ate so neatly today!" and "I think it was wonderful the way you shared your toys with Ethan." Praising his artwork, block towers, color or letter-recognition will all help to improve his self-esteem, but *you* will stand to benefit more from complimenting the *behaviors* you'd like him to repeat!

Try to be low-key, but consistent. It's harder to remember to always praise good behavior than it is to remember to criticize bad behavior. But criticism doesn't affect change in kids nearly as effectively as praise does, so make it a habit to praise behavior you like.

Try to match your praise to your child's excitement level. If she proudly says, "Look, Mommy! I cleaned my room!" then she deserves for you to share in her obvious pleasure over her accomplishment. If she's drawing a picture, and leaves it on the table to start playing with something that suddenly became more interesting to her, you may not need to gush compliments about that particular picture. If you praise too much and too heartily, your compliments could lose some of their value for your child. And if your praise is insincere, she'll know, and she'll lose trust in you.

Try this exercise from Dr. Sears: "Write down how many times you praised and how many times you criticized your child in the last twenty-four hours. We call these pull-ups and put-downs. If your pull-ups don't significantly outnumber your put-downs, you are shaping your child in the wrong direction."

70.

Teach voice modulation in a fun way.

Toddlers are loud, mostly when you don't want them to be. Some parents are super-sensitive to noisy public displays, while others seem practically oblivious to them. Whatever your threshold, you can do more than nag and plead to control your little opera star's volume.

Make it a game. When you're home and it doesn't matter, ask him to show you what his quiet voice and his loud voice sound like. Then talk about all the places where a quiet voice is best. Let him help you make the list of places like the library, restaurants, the home of your childless (on purpose) friends . . . Then talk about all the places where a loud voice is fine like the park, your backyard, the pool, playgroup. Depending on the rules of your household, you might want to deem loud voices acceptable in the bathtub or in his room, or even anywhere in the house except for during dinnertime.

After you've made your list, quiz him about which voice he would use in each spot. Make it fun. Yell and whisper at appropriate points in the conversation. Quiz him frequently over the next few days, as long as he enjoys the game.

Then, the next time you walk into a restaurant, tell him, "I've forgotten? What kind of voice should we use in here?" He'll be proud to know the answer, and more likely to comply. If he starts getting loud anyway, say, "Are we in the park? Are we in the pool?" Your silliness will remind him of the game, and make it more likely he'll quiet down than if you just did your old "Hush!" routine.

When all else fails and your toddler is on the verge of shattering crystal with his screams—fun screams, angry screams, or for-the-heck-of-it screams—try whispering or speaking very softly, in a calm, soothing manner. He might stop screaming out of curiosity because he can't hear what you're saying any other way. If he's upset, encourage him to say in words what's bothering him, but don't try to reason with him about it. Just be sympathetic. Whisper, "I know it's hard . . . " Try to hold him, but if he flails away, stay close by in case he changes his mind.

71.

Accept offers of help, even when they aren't helpful

Helping you do your grown-up stuff will make your toddler feel big and important. Allowing him to "help" will often mean more work for you initially but if you hang in there he'll eventually learn how to do things better. Toddlers will probably be willing to try to help you do just about anything, but some tasks will be more fun and doable for them than others.

If he asks to help you clean, let him. Who knows? You could train him to be a great duster, sweeper, or clutter-picker-upper. It's easy for a toddler to unload unbreakable storage containers from the dishwasher and put them in a low cabinet. And by two and a half, Tuck could do a pretty successful job of sorting the just-washed spoons, forks and knives (dull, flatwear knives) into their spots in the drawer.

A few of his other favorites are finding Mommy's shoes when we're going somewhere and holding the door open for me when I'm bringing in groceries. I know these jobs boost his confidence and help to make him feel included in the grown-up world. I always comment on what a great team we are and what wonderful stuff we can do when we work together. To encourage helpfulness in your toddler, read him *I Help Mommy* and *I Help Daddy*, published by Lowell House.

72.

Share the fun of your laundry.

Tuck actually gets excited when he hears the word, "laundry." He runs to his room to get his little hamper, which he drags to the laundry room. I bring the rest of the dirty stuff and set him up in his position on the dryer next to the washing machine. He turns the buttons, pours in the detergent, and watches the water rush in. As if this weren't exciting enough, I then start throwing clothes at him, which he gleefully catches, knowing it's his job to toss them into the machine.

Later, I hand him the wet clothes so he can load them into the dryer and turn it on. And then, the grand finale! We unload the dryer into a laundry basket, carry it into the living room, and dump all those warm, nice-smelling clothes and linens in the middle of the floor where we can roll in them and toss them and hide in them until the warm wears off.

He even loves the folding part. Toddlers can learn to fold washcloths. It's great for their egos and can actually be a help to you! Show your child how it's done, saying something like, "Pick up the bottom corners. Bring them up to meet their friends at the top. This corner says 'hi' to one top corner, and this corner says 'hi' to the other top corner. Smooth down the fold. Now, these corners on this side want to visit their friends on the other side, so bring them over like this . . . "

Sorting socks can be educational, too. Gather all the socks in a pile and see if your child can find the pairs. If you want to make more games out of the laundry, ask him to make a pile of all the red clothes, or all the underwear. After everything's folded, let him help you sort it into groups according to wearer.

Then, as the final laundry activity, use his wagon to pull the clothes through the house, dropping off each item in its proper destination.

73.

Encourage "all by self!" dressing.

I know it's faster for you to dress him, but when he starts showing all the signs of wanting to dress himself, take the time to help him learn. Most toddlers feel very proud of such a grown-up accomplishment.

Show him how to tell the front from the back by looking for tags. Or if, like Tucker, your child has long ago insisted that all labels be clipped off to avoid their ouchiness, use a laundry pen to mark the inside back collar of each shirt or dress. If you ever have problems deciding which of your children certain articles of clothing belong to, write the child's name back there. If not, you could draw a star, a smiley-face or some other symbol your toddler likes. Or, get started with letter-recognition and make a B for back. For underwear, you can teach boys that that funny pocket always goes in the front. For girls, you can make it a rule to only buy underwear with a picture or bow on the front so she won't get confused, or mark her undies with your laundry pen.

All those clothing fasteners can be extra-tricky, but they're irresistible to toddlers. Buy a book or toy that offers practice in zipping, buttoning, snapping, tying laces, pressing Velcro together, etc. But test it yourself first. A lot of those products are much harder to use than the real clothes! If you can't find a book or toy you like, just let your child practice on a few of his or your actual clothes when nobody's wearing them. Or make a toy yourself by putting a jacket on a big teddy bear and letting your child zip it up.

For buttons and snaps, demonstrate the bottom-up rule. Show your toddler how to start with the bottom button and the bottom button-hole, then move up to the next one, etc. Demonstrate how to hold the zipper away from the skin during zipping (especially for little boys who will soon be zipping in a very sensitive area!)

Shoes are often the hardest and last to master. To a toddler, the appropriate shoe for the foot he's targeting is whichever one he picks up first. Help him differentiate between right and left by using that laundry pen again—this time to draw a picture inside each shoe on the side that faces in. Then, teach him that his big toe should slide past the picture on its way into the shoe. To make it even easier to remember, draw the big toe. Or draw a foot in the bottom of the shoe, with a big, exaggerated big toe in the inside portion. Some shoes make it easy by having pictures on the outer sides only.

74.

Teach your child to give and receive compliments.

One sign of good self-esteem in people of any age is the ability to sincerely compliment others and the ability to gracefully accept the compliments they receive. Habits that form during the toddler years often stick for some time, so make it a point to compliment your toddler often and sincerely. Try to pick areas where the child is likely to agree with your assessment instead of focusing exclusively on "boosting" his confidence in areas he doesn't excel in.

You won't have to teach him to give compliments. Your modeling will be all the instruction he needs. You can smile and give *yourself* a private little compliment when you hear him saying to the next door neighbor, "Nice throw!"

Accepting compliments is another one of those areas where your modeling makes all the difference. If you are the sort of person who shrugs off the kind words spoken to you, it's likely your child will be likewise unable to accept a compliment. So take a look at yourself and brush up your own self-image if you want your child to feel good about his.

75.

Don't dwell!

I can't stand listening to parents yap, yap, yap at their kids about how horrible they are. It does nothing to correct the behavior and wears away at a child's self-esteem so badly that he has no motivation to behave any better. Toddlers respond best to calm, consistent redirection from loving caregivers.

If the child's behavior needs correcting, don't harp on it, and don't try to talk him into doing it your way. Take swift, authoritative action to stop it. If he's doing damage with a particular toy, take it away without a lot of fuss. If he's doing something he shouldn't be doing and won't stop, take him to a time-out spot. Don't yell or punish or give him much attention. Just quickly and boringly stop the misbehavior.

If he screams and tantrums, which is likely, be kind but not overly sympathetic. Tell him it's okay to feel mad and he can cry if he wants. Then go about your business and let him know he's welcome to join you when he's feeling better.

I love this example from John Rosemond's Making the "Terrible" Two's Terrific!

> "Don't use fifty words when five will do . . . a two-year-old who's climbing on a table will understand a firm 'Get down,' but will not understand, 'Sweetie, you need to get down from the table because you could fall and hurt yourself and we might have to take you to the doctor and that would make Mommy sad because I don't like to see my little boy hurt, okay?'
>
> In this case, the child will only hear, 'Gibberish table, gibberish fall, more gibberish doctor, blah, blah, blah, Mommy, goombah hurt.' He'll translate: The table fell on the doctor and Mommy got hurt. So, do yourself and your child a favor and keep it to 'Get down.'"

After you have corrected the behavior, offer a simple, direct reason for your actions, like, "Climbing on that table is dangerous."

76.

Know when NOT to say "please."

Using "please" and other nice words like it is the best way to encourage your child to use them. If everyone's in a pretty good mood and you're asking for your child's help with something, say, "Please bring me that cup." That's the good way to model "please."

But the word "please" should usually be avoided when disciplining your child. Let's say you've asked little Timmy to come to the table for dinner and he says, "No! Play cars!" while glaring at you from across the room. Whatever you do, don't get into a dialogue like, "Please come to the table, Timmy. Your dinner will be cold if you don't come now. Mommy made your favorite. Please be a good boy and . . . blah, blah, blah." All Timmy hears in this plea is lots of extra attention from Mommy. Mommy really wants him to come, but she's basically admitting she can't make him. Wow, that feels powerful. That feels so good that Timmy decides he'll just sit there playing with his cars forever.

Instead, say, "It's time for dinner now, Timmy. Come wash your hands." If Timmy says, "No! Play cars!", then set a timer for two or three minutes and tell him he can play with his cars until the timer goes off and then he has to put the cars away. (If this is a recurring problem, you'll soon figure out that you need to invite him to the table before you're actually ready to eat.)

Then, if the timer goes off and he still won't cooperate, calmly put the cars away, out of his reach, yourself. Tell him it's eating time now. If he's yelling about it, tell him that you'll help him wash his hands whenever he's ready. Then go back to your dinner and let him blow off steam until he tires of it and wants to join you. The less he can engage you in the drama of the situation the less rewarding it will be for him and the sooner he'll drop it.

77.

Give reminders to repeat offenders.

If you find yourself disciplining a particular issue over and over, anticipate the problem and warn your child in advance what the consequence will be. While everyone is still in a good mood, just before the misbehavior is likely to strike, offer a gentle reminder.

Say every single time your toddler plays outside she tries to pick your next-door neighbor's newly planted tulips. As you're walking out the door tell her, "I know that you like to look at Ms. Fisher's flowers and that you know not to pick them. But if you forget and you try to pick a flower, we will come back in the house and you won't get to play outside." Say it matter-of-factly, not ominously or threateningly, like it's just a basic law of the universe. Of course, distract her away from the danger zone as much as you can and praise her for playing nicely in her own yard.

But if the temptation becomes too great, and she makes a run for the flowerbed, stop her at the point at which it's clear she's about to yank her prize out of the ground. Pick her up and bring her in the house, saying, "Since you tried to pick a flower, we'll have to go in now." She may scream and kick and protest and it may take many incidents like this to curb the behavior, but eventually she'll stop pilfering flowers.

78.

Get your child to do what you want her to do.

When you want your child to do something, and she refuses (as any normal toddler will occasionally do) try John Rosemond's strategic opportunity method. First, with kind but firm authority, tell your child what she is to do. "It's time for you to pick up your toys now, dear."

If she ignores the request, instead of harping, go do your own thing and don't pay her much attention. Soon she will need you. She will want you to play, or she'll want juice, or she'll want to "help" you chop those vegetables. That's when you say, again firmly, "Yes, you may have some juice, but first you must pick up your toys." For this to work, you have to stay nonchalant. If you try to prove your authority over her, it will backfire. Toddlers just hate that.

Let her consider her options. She wants the juice, and Mommy seems to be saying that the basic law of the universe is that picking up toys must proceed juice drinking. *Hmmm.* This way, the decision is still hers. She can do what you want her to without losing too much face. I've found this method to work great on those rare occasions when we're lolling about on a Sunday afternoon with no pressing engagements (in other words, about twice a year). So I share it with you in the hopes that you are a wiser parent than I am and you have many more unscheduled hours in your day-to-day life than I have in mine.

79.

Expect testing.

Every parent of a toddler complains about the incessant habit these children have of testing their parents. "Testing" goes by some other not-as-nice names like "defiance," and "stubbornness," but it basically boils down to the child purposefully doing the opposite of whatever it is the parent wants her to do.

According to John Rosemond,

> Any child can be counted upon to test any rule. Testing is a child's only way of discovering whether, in fact, the rule truly exists. Telling the child 'This is a rule' isn't convincing enough. Children—especially young ones—are concrete thinkers. Rules must be *demonstrated*. So, when a child breaks a rule, parents have an obligation to impose some form of discipline. This gets the child's attention and says, 'See? We were telling you the truth.' So, parents demonstrate their reliability by being consistent. The more a child knows he can rely upon his parents, the more secure the child will feel.

> If, on the other hand, a child breaks a stated rule, and instead of *doing something assertive*, parents threaten or talk themselves blue in the face or get excited but don't do anything, the child is forced to test the rule again. And again. And again. Testing of this sort 'spins the child's wheels.' It wastes time and energy the child could otherwise use in creative, constructive activity. Consistency frees children from the burden of having to test rules repeatedly. Therefore, consistency helps children become all they are capable of becoming.

As previously acknowledged, being consistent doesn't mean you have to handle every broken rule with the exact same response. The important thing is consistency of *attitude*. If you are always calm, firm, and matter-of-fact about the consequences of your toddler's misbehavior, he'll get a clear picture of what is expected of him. He'll start to control himself more, and that's the first step toward figuring out how to discipline *himself*.

80.

Give answers to WHY?

Why, why, why do toddlers never tire of asking WHY? No parent—not even a Jeapordy-contestant parent—could possibly know the correct answers to all those inquiries. The good news is that your answers do not have to be correct. You will not raise a dullard if you fail to explain the chemical intricacies of oxidation to a two-year-old who wants to know why his metal toy truck turned brown when it was left in the backyard for two months. If you happen to be well-versed in chemistry, it won't hurt to have a go at it, but it's also fine to say, "Because it rained on the truck and that's what happens when metal gets rained on."

It's also okay to make something up. Maybe the truck has been on a magical adventure and changing colors was part of the magic. Maybe it was tired of being blue and decided to become brown instead. If you routinely engage in fantasy-play with your child, he'll likely be thrilled with these answers, and want to elaborate on the fantasy with you. He'll know, of course, that your conversation has shifted into make-believe-mode, but he probably won't mind. The important thing it that you always provide some answer, since most WHYs are primarily an attempt to engage you in conversation. It's okay to turn the tables occasionally, too, and say, "Why do YOU think it turned brown?"

When the WHYs drive you crazy, keep in mind that asking WHY is a sign of intelligence in a toddler. He uses WHY to get information, but also to explore cause-and-effect. He asks, you answer. He's not looking so much for the actual reason for something, but just confirming that a reason exists, and that you're willing to provide it. Giving an answer that makes some sort of sense to him (even if it's make-believe) is kinder than giving an answer that is impossible for him to comprehend. There's plenty of time to teach him more accurate information when he's better able to assimilate it.

81.

Let a clinger cling.

It's happened to all of my toddler-parent friends at one time or another. That independent toddler who's been running away from parents in stores and parks and doing everything she can possibly do "by self!" suddenly wants to be in arms all day long. She hides behind her mother's legs and begs to be picked up and screams at the very mention of her favorite sitter's name. "We're having a mommy-day," Robyn tells me on the phone, and I know exactly what she means.

The experts say temporary clinginess during toddlerhood is absolutely normal and nothing to worry about. It's just the way independence naturally evolves, in a two-steps-forward, one-step-back dance that has a secret rhythm all its own. Often, the dependency streak follows some grand show of independence, as if the child needs to retreat back into the zone of super-security to rest and refuel for the next big step forward.

When your toddler wants you and nothing and no one else, try to allow it. If you push her away you'll threaten her comfort zone, making her insecure and even more determined to cling to you. As a child realizes that she is separate from her parents and can have an identity apart from them, she alternates between feeling exhilarated with the realization and feeling terrified by it. She has a natural, strong drive to become her own person, but can only comfortably do so when she knows for sure that you'll always be there as her safety net. Her clingy times are your chance to prove it to her. Pick her up, cuddle her like you did when she was an infant, and let her see that you enjoy this period of more intense interaction. Once she's convinced, she'll be happily off on her own again.

I'm a huge believer in baby slings and big old Tuck still sits happily in his when we're out somewhere doing a lot of walking; but for around the house I have another contraption called a Hip Hiker that helps immensely. Toddlers are heavy to lug in any fashion, but the Hip Hiker provides a little shelf that extends from your waist for a toddler to sit on when he's just dying to be next to you all day. It puts no strain on your neck or back, so it's pretty comfortable. (Call 1-800-321-7956 to get one.)

Of course, any abrupt change in your toddler's behavior warrants some inspection. If focused attention from you doesn't cheer her up, you'll want to look closely at what's going on in her life that might be causing her undue stress.

82.

Don't fear the fears.

Parents often worry that their toddlers' irrational fears are indications of psychological problems or worse. But psychologists say that intense fears are extremely common for the age group. Most are symbolic of the child's growing detachment from the parents. The more he stands on his own, the more he'll have to handle anxiety by himself. The monsters and ghosts are expressions of his vulnerability.

The very fact that the words for imaginary scary things exist is one cause of the problem. Children hear about monsters and witches and ghosts and nasty spells in the context of make-believe. But to a toddler, there is no comprehending how a word could exist for a thing that does not. Therefore, if there is a word and the toddler is made aware of the meaning of the word, the thing exists. He can't see it any other way.

Likewise, if a toddler can imagine something, it exists. He can conjure up an image of Daddy when Daddy is at work, and he can conjure up an image of an evil octopus in his closet. He can't yet understand why one is any less real than the other.

83.

Fix the fear by entering its world.

There is no point in reasoning with a child who has an irrational fear. Telling him there's nothing to be afraid of will get you nowhere. Dismissing his fear will give him the message that you're not interested in helping him; he's on his own. Since his feelings of vulnerability are what caused the fear in the first place, taking this course will only elevate the fear to phobic proportions.

So acknowledge the existence of the fear. That's not the same as saying, "Yes, you're right. There is an evil octopus in your closet." Try something like, "I know you're feeling very scared because you're imagining an octopus in your closet. When I was your age, I had scary thoughts like that, too." Then, fight fire with fire. Tell him, "You know what I'm imagining right now? I see a big, beautiful whale standing guard at the foot of your bed. She's much bigger than that octopus, and stronger too. She wants to protect you while you sleep. That whale will keep you very safe. Do you see her?" According to toddler logic, if you put an imaginary whale in his room, it's there. He can't deny its existence without blowing his whole octopus thing at the same time.

Some mommies and daddies have come up with "monster spray" that keeps those under-bed dwellers at bay. The point is to work with your child. You know his likes and dislikes, what he's currently impressed with. What hero can he imagine that will be a worthy opponent for the villains he's imagining? Help him find and solidify that hero so he can use it to his advantage.

Fear of the dark is epidemic in toddlerworld. Some adults even share this fear, so it's one that parents can more readily accept. Dr. Sears recommends,

> The principle of gradually increasing exposure helps the child overcome fear of the dark. Play dark tag, beginning with the lights on in a room that preferably has a dimmer switch so that you can gradually dim the lights. Play hide-and-seek at dusk, and let the game extend into the darkness. Play follow the leader as you weave around the yard at night on an exploring expedition. Initially, hold your child's hand as you explore together. Give your child his own flashlight to keep next to his bed so that he can turn it on to shed some

light onto suspicious piles of clothing that turn into "a bear" when there's only a night-light. Sometimes just knowing that he has the power to change the darkness into light is enough to quell the fear. Or just leave more light on in his room; it won't interfere with his ability to sleep. He'll start turning it off himself when he's older.

84.

Don't over-condemn aggressiveness.

Whenever I see a toddler hit a playmate in a playgroup, my heart goes out—not to the small victim—but to the poor mother of the clobberer. Nothing is so wrenching as seeing one's precious angel act like pure devil in front of other people. Even though everyone has been told that toddlers just act that way sometimes, the implication is always there—wafting about the room—that you have done something amiss in raising your child or that your little darling is just a bad seed.

For the record, John Rosemond reminds us once again, that:

> Aggressive children don't have bad parents, nor is anything *wrong* with them. Most aggressive behavior—no matter how "uncivilized" (biting, for example)—is *normal*. Some children are simply more inclined toward aggressive behavior than others. We refer to this inclination with the words *heredity, predisposition,* and *temperament.* In any case, it boils down to "they were (probably) born that way."
>
> Some toddlers, more passively disposed, when a toy they're playing with is snatched, will sit

helplessly and cry. There's nothing *wrong* with these children for crying. They were born that way. Other toddlers, more aggressively disposed, when a toy is snatched, will snatch back and clobber. These aren't *bad* children. There's nothing *wrong* with them, either. They, too, were born that way. Remember, it takes all kinds.

Even though most parents have heard some information along those lines time and time again, they still tend to overreact when a toddler bites, kicks, or hits. It's just so darn hard to see that kind of behavior in our children. But while aggression should never be ignored, it does require a special kind of discipline. The tendency toward aggression is very difficult to correct completely. It usually is never fully resolved until the child outgrows it. But a responsible parent must ALWAYS intervene when her child acts aggressively.

As soon as the act occurs, calmly and matter-of-factly separate the two children. First, comfort the injured party. By letting your child see your concern for his victim you'll be modeling compassion and empathy—important concepts for him to absorb along his path to non-aggressive behavior. Look your child in the eyes and say, "No hitting. Hitting hurts." (or no biting, scratching, etc.).

Without hesitation or too much reprimanding, take your child away from the scene of the crime and impose your pre-established time-out ritual. There is a difficult line to walk here. You must always take action to correct aggressive behavior, but you also must be careful not to overreact. Whenever you overreact to a behavior, you run the risk of inadvertently increasing it.

Shimm and Ballen write,

> Remember, you don't have a monster just because your toddler bites or hits. Neither is a cardinal sin. Biting didn't start out as an antisocial activity. It's a natural progression from sucking, gumming, hugging. Your toddler also really might not know that socking someone on the arm is not an appropriate way to greet people.

If parents don't overreact, a toddler will probably have a short career as a biter and hitter. Try saying calmly and seriously: "I can't let you hurt Caroline. But I will also not let anyone hurt you. You can tell me when you are angry."

Toddlers love the chance to boss someone else around. It could be a pet, a younger toddler, or even their stuffed animals. They get to be you with all that control you have and make someone else be them, with all their powerlessness. If no one's getting hurt, ignore these power trips and chalk them up to a passing developmental stage.

85.

Correct aggression CAREFULLY.

As painful as it is to watch our angels turn violent, it's equally painful when you're the parent of the clobbered. Nothing can turn mommy-friends against one another faster than mishandled violence between toddlers. If yours hits, bites, or pushes, by all means be apologetic and show concern for the victim. And if yours is the victim, try to summon up some understanding and forgiveness. It's easy to feel smug, like your child is better, sweeter, and more sensitive than the aggressive child, but the situation is rarely as clear-cut as it looks. Toddlers go through many phases, and next week, or with another playmate, you may find that the situation is reversed.

Tucker has many friends of similar age and he's always made me proud with his ability to happily co-exist in playdates with them. His very favorite friend, however, is Emily—the proverbial girl next door—a petite, gentle angel six months younger than Tuck. Since our two families are very friendly and my husband and I love Emily, it pained me to no end when Tuck began bopping her, pushing her down, and ripping toys out her hands with startling regularity. Shocked to see him behaving this way, Emily's mother and I both reacted strongly to the first few transgressions, and our interference got even more dramatic as his domination became habitual.

I was baffled. He was never overly-aggressive with his other friends. I knew that he truly loved this girl, always delighted in seeing her . . . what was the problem? Eventually, Emily's mom and I came to understand that a combination of factors was probably at work.

First of all, I know now in retrospect that my strong interference exacerbated his tendencies. With his other toddler friends, the moms pretty much left the kids to work out their own toy squabbles, getting involved only when truly necessary. The kids were more-or-less equal in size and heft, and no one ever got too maligned or riled up. My reaction was very different in the situation with Emily. When Tuck saw that taking toys from Emily could bring mommy-conversations to an abrupt halt and get both mommies to focus so much exciting attention on the toddlers, taking toys from her became all the more irresistible to him.

Another factor was probably his level of familiarity with Emily. Since she's right next door, he sees her far more frequently than he sees his other friends. Siblings are known to be much more violent with one another than playmates, and his day-to-day relationship with Emily is closer to a sibling relationship than any of his other friendships.

Also, she's little. We don't like to think our sweet children would take advantage of such discrepancies, but in toddlerworld, the laws of the jungle apply. The deliciousness of being bigger and stronger than someone else when you've always been the smallest in your family just tempts some kids into testing their superior strength. Her size and naturally passive temperament made her an easy target.

John Rosemond says,

> Expect real trouble . . . when passive toddlers are mixed with active, aggressive ones. The more assertive toddlers, sensing the advantage, will take it. The result: snatching, hitting, and perhaps even biting, all the tune of a chorus of wails from the more passive children. In such instances, the worst thing supervising adults can do is punish the assertive children and comfort the passive ones. Refereeing of this sort will only make the conflict more intense, the imbalance more pronounced. Managing mismatches among young children demands that an adult get involved, at least temporarily, as a facilitator, a mediator, a "Peacemaker of the Sandbox."

When Emily's mom and I changed course a little the situation improved quite a bit, though he'd still bop Emily before he'd bop any of his other friends. Then again, he's still in the throws of being two, while Emily has yet to hit that mark. Perhaps when Emily is two and a half and Tuck has moved into the more mellow three-stage, the tables will turn.

86.

Rally the underdog.

If your child is passive, you may have a hard time seeing her shoved and bullied by her more assertive playmates. As tempting as it is to rush to her defense, John Rosemond maintains it's to her benefit for you to stay as removed as possible. Until *she* sees the situation as a problem, she won't be able to do anything about it. Too much interference from you could make the situation worse in the long run. She may start looking to you to solve all her crises instead of working out her own solutions.

Shimm and Ballen suggest coaching the child to stand up for herself. A parent could say, "Hold on tight when Suzanne tries to take your ball. Tell her, 'It's mine.'" They demonstrate:

> The dialogue below is an example of how a parent can empower both the aggressive and the cautious toddler. The parent shows in a nonjudgmental way that he or she understands how the child is feeling and then gives the child words so that she can express her own feelings.
>
> Bully: Give me that bucket now. I need it now. (Without waiting a second she grabs the bucket from Matthew and runs away.)
>
> Parent: Sara, I see you took that bucket that Matthew was playing with.
>
> Bully: I want it.
>
> Parent: As soon as you are finished, give it back.
>
> Bully: No, I need it.

Parent: I know you need it. But will you be finished soon? (By asking the aggressor if she's finished, the parent is giving her a chance to save face and give back the toy.)

Parent (to victim): Say, "It's mine." You can be angry Sara took your bucket. Next time hold on tight and say, "It's mine." You can tell her.

What usually happens at this point is that the aggressor throws the toy to the victim. She isn't made to feel ashamed, so she can show a little empathy for others. Meanwhile, the satisfied victim gets a glimmer of understanding: "Hey, I can handle this. It does work to hold on."

87.

Know how hard it is to suddenly be the big sibling

If you have a new baby while your child is still a toddler, you need to be fully prepared that it will be hard on your toddler. You will want her to be just as happy and full of love for this new family member as you and your spouse are, but it simply is not within her capacity to fulfill this expectation.

There will surely be moments of pride and tender feelings, but there will also surely be moments of intense jealousy. Try not to get angry with your toddler. Involve her as much as possible with the care of the new baby and keep her daily routine as much like her pre-baby routine as you can. Don't be surprised if she regresses to some of her own "baby" behaviors. Indulge her and shower her with as much of your love and attention as you can spare.

Shimm and Ballen say,

> Your toddler is going to have passionate and turbulent emotions toward you, the baby, and just about every human being she comes in contact with. You can't ignore the feelings your toddler will have of being displaced by this tiny

intruder. Painful as it is, your toddler is going to feel squeezed out.

You have to allow these feelings of hatred, jealousy, and rage. At the same time, of course, your toddler will have feelings of love and pride and will share in the happiness of having a new family member. It is extremely important to let your child know that he can have any thoughts he wants and that you will still love him. You don't want your toddler to grow up feeling bad about having "bad" feelings. Your toddler needs to know that bad feelings won't destroy his parents or him.

When your toddler stalks away from you and slams her bedroom door, try saying something like, "Even when you are angry at Mommy, she still loves you." When your toddlers screams, "I hate you" at the baby, lightly say: "Sometimes you like your sister, and sometimes you don't. You seem to be having a hard time because I'm feeding her rather than playing with you." . . . Letting toddlers know that their feelings can change helps them to be less afraid of their "bad" feelings.

My friend Julie recently gave birth to her second son and was feeling frustrated by her toddler's increasing demands on her time. She felt she was doing everything she could to minimize sibling rivalry, but Luke was sulky and irritable whenever she spent time with his new brother, Liam. Then a sudden flash of realization struck her. She says, "I'm the one who had a new baby, not Luke. I now have two favorite people, but for Luke, I'm still his one and only favorite person. No wonder he doesn't want to share me."

88.

Cut off the payoff.

There is one fascinating behavioral tidbit that you may remember from your psychology classes that is particularly helpful to keep in mind when disciplining your toddler. Do you recall what B.F. Skinner figured out with those rats in that box of his?

John C. Friel, Ph.D. and Linda D. Friel, M.A. explain in *The 7 Worst Things Parents Can Do*,

> He put a rat into what is now known as a Skinner Box—a box with a lever and a food dispenser on one wall—and then guess what happened? That's right. Because rats are naturally curious and because they naturally get up on their haunches and poke around with their little paws, the rat accidentally, but eventually, pressed the lever; and lo and behold, a food pellet was dispensed and the hungry rat got his first taste of the exciting world of cause and effect.

It didn't take the rat long to master this cause-and-effect progression that Skinner called "operant conditioning". Then Skinner became stingier with the food pellets. He discovered that if the rat had to press the lever several times before he got the pellet, the rat's lever-pressing behavior became much stronger. The biggest discovery was that if the pellet was dispensed only randomly (kind of like the payoffs from a slot machine) the behavior was strongest of all.

I don't mean to make any comparisons between your toddler and a rat, but psychology has accepted these principals of operant conditioning to apply to human beings and they help explain gambling addictions as well as other human tendencies. So let's see if we can apply this knowledge to our parenting practices. If your toddler whines and begs for candy at the checkout counter and you always say yes, the whining and begging probably will never get too intense or out of hand. If, on the other hand, you say yes only after repeated whines and entreaties, you can expect the whining to be a little louder and stronger. And, if you rarely but *occasionally* say yes, you can expect the whining and begging to be about as intense and annoying as it can be, every single time you get in that checkout line.

Luckily, there is a solution. Skinner's research shows that the best way to extinguish a behavior is to stop reinforcing it. When he turned off the power to the food dispenser, the rat eventually stopped pressing the lever. But *before* the behavior was extinguished, the rat went through a period of pushing that lever like there was no tomorrow. Since the payoff had been so intermittent, it took a long time before he was convinced that the rewards had truly ceased to exist.

And unfortunately, that's what you can probably expect from your toddler, too. If you've been randomly rewarding tantrums or whining or defiance or any other negative behavior, it won't be an easy road to eradicating that behavior. The Friels go on to explain,

> If at any time during this gradual extinction process, you reinforce that rat for pulling the lever even once, its rate of lever-pulling behavior increases dramatically, often to levels stronger than before . . . Once you remove the reinforcement for a behavior, you must keep it removed. There are no ifs, ands, buts, exceptions, special occasions or soothings of our neurotic consciences. "No" means "no."

> What sometimes happens is that after a couple of successful weeks, many of us tend to backslide, as if to say, "This extinction stuff really works. It's been three weeks and my daughter hasn't had one tantrum! She's been so good! I feel a little guilty about all the struggling she's had to do. Maybe I'll buy her some candy at the checkout counter!" If you feel like doing this, please stop yourself and remember that it would be both cruel and confusing to her to do it.

Continuing with the checkout counter example, remember that it is the whining and begging *in this specific situation* that you are trying to eradicate. Trying to eliminate all whining at once might be overwhelming for both you and your child. And remember also that it does not mean your child can never again eat candy. Depending on your particular goals for her sweets-consumption, she could still eat candy at birthday parties, or even eat candy that you buy and surprise her with. But you could never again buy candy at the checkout counter without nullifying all your hard work. Since this behavior-extinguishing technique is so absolute, save it for behaviors that are really driving you crazy, and never try to extinguish more than one behavior at a time.

Read, read, read to him!

You've probably been reading to your child ever since he was a dime-sized fetus, but even if you haven't—especially if you haven't!—the toddler years are an essential time to encourage a love of books. Most toddlers like to read the same books over and over again. They enjoy board books, rhyming stories, colorful illustrations as well as photographs, and books with exciting pop-ups, pull-tabs and flaps to lift.

At this stage, reading should just be for fun. Don't ever force books on your toddler. Even if it takes you many attempts to get to the last page of a story, never persuade him to continue listening if he'd rather build a block tower. Get to know the length of his average attention span and look for books that can fit into it. If he shows interest in a book that contains more text than he enjoys, just turn each page and look at and briefly discuss each of the pictures for a while. That will give him a chance to love the book and get familiar with it. Once that happens, you might start reading more and more of the actual text until he happily wants to hear it all.

Don't be surprised if he wants to hear the same story twenty times in a row. He might start to remember the words, especially if they rhyme. Give him a chance to "read" with you. You can say, "The eensy weensy . . . " and point your finger to the word spider while he chimes in, "spider!" Then you say, "climbs up the water . . . " and point to the word while he says "spout!".

Some families like to set aside a special time for reading every day and for many, that's bedtime. I find that too limiting and prefer to make reading a fun activity that we do whenever the mood strikes, which is usually a few times a day. Our friends like to keep books in a special place and make sure kids respect them as fragile and valuable. That works great for their kids, but for other children who have a hard time being gentle it can be a turn-off. We keep our books in every toy box and every nook and drawer all over the house, so there's always a good book handy to grab and read wherever we are. We have books in the car . . . books in the wagon that he looks at while he's pulled around the block . . . we even have plastic books in the bathtub.

The one big exception to our books-all-over rule is library books. They go on a special shelf and Tucker knows we have to be very gentle with them so other kids can read them after we're done with them. We know our library books are "sharing books" and that makes them a little more special. Our library book shelf also helps us to always know where these special books are when it's time to bring them back.

Taking the time to read with your child and make reading fun is one of the best things you'll ever do for him. Sharing reading time each day will lead to closer communication between you on many levels. Always stop and talk about what you're reading. Don't make it a no-no to interrupt the reading with questions or comments about what's being read. Listening to your child talk about his observations in books will give you lots of insight into the things he's concerned about. Let books solidify the connection between the two of you, and you may discover that these shared reading times are as meaningful to you as they are to your child.

90.

Take advantage of the library!

If the library isn't one of your child's favorite places by now, what are you waiting for? Most libraries offer awesome, FREE programs for kids of different ages, and many include storytimes for toddlers. But even if yours doesn't, you might want to set aside a certain hour of a certain day of the week as LIBRARY TIME for you and your child. Visiting the library on a regular basis now will make it a familiar and comfortable place that she'll be happy to return to throughout her school years.

If you're planning your first visit, present the idea with as much enthusiasm as you would if you were taking your toddler to a fabulous new park. Tell her what she can expect, make a fun game of using "library voices," and decide on the way there how many books she can check out. My local library has suggested "10 books for 10 toes," or "five books for five fingers" or later, as she grows, one book for every year of her age.

See if your library will issue your child her own library card. Libraries vary in their policies about how old a child must be for this. If she can get her own card, explain to her how she can use it. A typically power-hungry toddler will love having a magic card with her name on it that can get her books to bring home. Even if the card is in your name, let your child be the one to hand it over at the book check-out.

The library is the perfect place for a toddler to exercise her right to choose. As much as possible, let her make her own selections. If she's overwhelmed with the options, you might want to pre-select a few books and then let her make the final selections from those. The librarian can help you figure out which books are age-appropriate. Try not to discourage her picks, even if it's a book she already has at home, or one that she's checked out a lot already. She needs to feel some control over her book selection process.

You can always add a few books that you've selected for her. If she's developed a recent fascination with cats, find her a photographic non-fiction book on the subject. Tune into HER interests—monsters, Mars, or marbles.

But, while libraries offer a great opportunity to read a variety of books, the books from the library should always *accompany*, not *replace*, the books your child owns. According to *Raising a Reader*, by Paul Kropp,

> " . . . the books your child owns are the ones you'll read to him over and over again. And the books that are read to your child over and over again at ages two and three become the first books your child will read by himself at ages four and five. These are the books he will keep going back to, reading and re-reading, sometimes long after you'd think they'd be outgrown. One study says that some of the books on your child's bookshelf will be read more than 300 times before he begins to lose interest in them. This kind of repeated rereading is essential for building reading skills, but it can happen only when children have their own books."

91.

Prepare your toddler for reading-readiness.

It may seem like your toddler's reading days are far away but it's never too early to introduce some basic concepts that will give him a head-start when the time to read comes along.

When you read with your child, talk about the different parts of the books. Ask him what's on the "cover." As you turn the pages, say that you are turning pages . . . then eventually let him be the one to turn pages and congratulate him on his expert page-turning skills. Board books have the easiest pages to turn, so he'll probably master that long before he can effectively turn one paper page at a time.

Sometimes when you're reading to him, run your finger along under the text. That reinforces the idea that those squiggly black lines on the page actually hold the story. It also makes your child aware that text is read from the left side of the page to the right, and from the top row down. Knowing those concepts, which we completely take for granted, will give him a tremendous head start in the basics of reading.

92.

Help your older toddler begin to learn to write.

Since kids learn to draw pictures long before they learn to write, let your child draw a story on a piece of paper. Even if the image is unrecognizable to you, ask him what it is, then write his answer on the paper. Ask a few more questions, and a more fully formed story may unfold. Write it all down and let your child see that he has created the story. The important learning here is that ideas can be captured not only by pictures, but also by words, which can then be captured by writing on paper.

For more reinforcement with this, write your child notes. Tucker loves this already. I'll write a little message on a piece of paper with a simple little picture and leave it where he knows it's for him. He'll find it and excitedly demand that I read it. It can just be "Dear Tucker, Thank you for helping me bring the trash outside. Love, Mommy." He'll remember the message, save the note, and later when he sees it, he can "read" it back to me.

93.

Make a special book, all about your toddler.

As we've discussed, your toddler's favorite subject is probably HER! You can help her celebrate that wonderful topic by making a book all about her life.

Pick a normal, routine day. Do the things you always do, but keep a loaded camera nearby at all times. Snap a shot of her waking up, eating breakfast, getting dressed, playing with her favorite toys, going to the park or a playgroup, eating lunch . . . Don't concern yourself too much with getting the perfect, or most flattering photograph. Your job is to record the events, so approach the project like a photojournalist. Take the final picture of your sleeping angel in her bed that night.

If she attends a preschool or daycare, you have two options. You could pick an average weekend day when you're with her all day; or you could photograph her as she arrives at school, with her teacher, and again as you pick her up. If you think the teacher wouldn't mind, leave your camera and ask if she'd take a few shots throughout the day.

Once you've developed the roll, share the photos with your child and let her help you put them in chronological order. Assemble the book as elaborately as you'd like. Fashion pages from folded construction paper or poster board. Bind your pages with staples, or punch holes and thread your book together with ribbon. Attach the photos with glue stick, photo corners, or even tape. Just don't get so fancy that you exclude your child from the process. You want her to feel that the end result is largely her own creation.

Let her dictate the text to accompany each photograph as you record her words in the book. If your child is very young, maybe you'll want to write the words yourself or not write any words at all, letting the pictures tell the story.

Now she has a book she can really relate to! Let her read it to you, whether or not she even looks at any writing that's there. It's her story, so who better to tell it? She'll probably be proud of her creation and want to share it with all the important people in her life.

And just think . . . if it's not completely demolished from repeated readings, you'll have a priceless keepsake—a little slice of her life at that particular elusive stage she's living right now. You may want to repeat the process every year, or even half-year (be sure to date them!). Won't they be fun to pull out at her high school graduation party?

94.

Choose the right preschool.

If your child is not already attending a daycare center, you may be wondering when the best time would be for him to begin school of some sort. There is nothing wrong with keeping a child at home until he begins kindergarten. But since the majority of American children do begin their education before kindergarten, your child may lag behind his classmates in certain skills unless you make a point to prepare him yourself.

Most experts agree that three is the perfect age for a child to begin attending some sort of social setting without a parent around. At three, a child is ready to form real friendships with peers, and he's better able to appreciate concepts of sharing, taking turns, and delaying gratification.

According to Lawrence Kutner, a school with too rigorous an academic objective is not in a toddler's best interest. And neither is one with no formal curriculum whatsoever. He says:

> The most impressive preschools and kindergartens I've seen are those that take a developmental approach to early education. They integrate social skills with academic learning in ways that make the most of young children's abilities. While the curricula that developmentally based preschools use are well-defined, they are not always obvious to the casual observer. Instead of having a "lesson," they will weave their objectives into the children's activities.
>
> Such schools will often pick a topic for a week, such as "things that are alive," and approach it from many different directions, several times each day. The children may eat tomatoes and plant cucumber seeds in a small garden, play with a visiting puppy, take a trip to the zoo, and learn about why their doctor uses a stethoscope. This multifaceted approach allows preschoolers to experience the concept of "being alive" with all of their senses.

When considering a preschool, visit it frequently before making your decision. Go at different times of the day and observe how the teachers interact with the children. See how the transitions are handled in the morning. Do the teachers greet each child by name? Do they pay special attention to children who are having trouble separating? Are they treating the children the way you'd like your child to be treated?

Lawrence Kutner also recommends,

> Get references. Don't just ask for the names of a few parents. The teacher or center director will naturally try to put you in touch with those parents who are the happiest. Instead, ask for a list of all the parents of children in what would be your child's classroom. While you need not call them all, you're more likely to get a diversity of opinions—both compliments and brickbats— if you select people at random from the whole list.

> Talk to at least three parents of different children. Explain that you're considering the center for your child and would like their general opinion of it. Then ask some specific questions. How useful is the information they get about their children from the teachers? How often do teachers leave the school? (Early education has a higher turnover rate among employees than other fields. If this school is having more trouble with this than other schools in your city, that's a sign of a larger problem.)

95.

Ease the transition.

No matter how fabulous a preschool is, the first day is going to be tough for your child. Make it as easy as possible by preparing her as much as you can. Talk to her about the new school with excitement in your voice. Read her books about school like *Miss Bindergarten Gets Ready for Kindergarten* and *The Berenstain Bears Go to School.*

A friend of mine made a book for her daughter with roughly drawn sketches (I mean roughly!) all about her preschool. The most valuable thing about the book was that it showed, clearly, how the mother would be dropping her daughter off, LEAVING, and then RETURNING to get her after her daughter had enjoyed a fun time playing with friends and toys. Reading the book together many times before the big day allowed the child to fully comprehend and accept the fact that her mother would not be staying with her.

Most schools will allow you to visit with your toddler several times before the child starts. Take advantage of this, but make it clear that these visiting times are different from attending the school. Point out that the other kids don't have their mommies with them, and look how much fun they're having! Share this observation casually, and don't assume that your child will protest your leaving. Some children are fine alone right from the start, though the vast majority will cry initially. But if you act as though you expect her cry, you increase the odds that she will.

Some preschools will allow a parent to hang around as long as she'd like for the first few hours or days that a new child attends. But many others do not permit this since it can upset the other children who do not have parents there. If you can't remain in the room with your child, ask if you can watch her unobserved. Most preschools have video monitors or peepholes, or some pre-established way for parents to spy undetected. (If yours does not, and the administrator doesn't make you feel welcome to stay and observe, look for another school.)

If your child cries when you leave, watch from this secret spot until he is happily involved in class activities. Preschool teachers say that almost all children who seem inconsolable at a parent's departure do cheer up quickly once the parent is out of sight. You'll feel a lot better if you stick around to witness that, so try to arrange your schedule so that you don't have to rush away the second you leave him.

96.

Recognize a compliment in disguise.

Your toddler will probably dump on you. Recognize this behavior as the compliment that it really is, and you will spare yourself much emotional anguish. Here's a common scenario: A parent arrives to pick up a child from preschool. She's anxious to reconnect with her darling after a long workday. But as soon as the child sees her, he says, "Go away!" and starts to throw toys in an aggressive manner.

The mom is hurt and baffled. Has he suffered undue emotional stress at the school? Is she a bad parent for leaving him in this place? Her anguish is compounded when the teacher says, "He's been so sweet all day." While Mom is glad to hear that her son had a pleasant time, she now worries: Is he punishing her for leaving him? Does this indicate a future relationship between them that's strained and conflict-ridden?

Experts agree that behavior such as this is common and nothing to be alarmed about. Lawrence Kutner writes,

> Spending the day in a child-care setting, a preschool, or a kindergarten takes a lot of emotional control. Young children must suppress their urges to act impulsively and grab everything they want for themselves. There's a tremendous social pressure to share things, wait patiently in line, and do other things that don't come naturally to a toddler or preschooler. By the end of the day, a child has built up a tremendous amount of emotional tension.

> They can't express this tension with words, of course. Behavior is the language of childhood. They share their frustrations by asserting their power over their parents at the end of the day because their parents are the people they feel closest to. While they may endure some brief anger because of their behavior, they know that they will not be permanently rejected. It is a sign of how much stronger the relationship the child has with the parents than with the teachers.

The same kind of behavior can be seen when you've left your child with a sitter, a nanny, or even with doting grandparents. It's just human nature to save our worst selves for those we feel the most comfortable with. Adults do it, too. If you suffer a particularly stressful day at work, chances are you will successfully suppress your urge to strangle your boss, but you may come home in a foul mood and not feel better until you've thoroughly trashed her to your supportive husband who you know will be able to handle your rage and love you just the same. In less mature moments, many adults will take out their anger on their kids, spouses, or pets.

So recognize those trying episodes as tributes to the close bond you have established with your child, and try to be indulgent of them. Allow plenty of time for transitions, respond with patience and love, and your child will soon be done venting and ready for connecting.

97.

Consider skipping punishments altogether.

Toddlers—even older toddlers—should not be punished with consequences that are not immediately apparent. If your child runs away from you at the grocery store and you tell him, "Because you did that, you cannot play outside after dinner tonight," he will feel no immediate consequence to his actions. Even if he plays outside after dinner every night, he will not feel any loss at the particular moment that you issue your punishment. He will probably cry, but his sadness will be a response to your anger at him more than disappointment over his sentence.

And then, to remain true to your word, you will have to prohibit him playing outside after dinner. What if he has been a perfect angel the whole rest of the afternoon and through dinnertime? Carrying out your stated punishment will mean bringing up the whole misbehavior incident again, in effect punishing him twice.

A better course would have been to implement a consequence that is directly related to the crime. Warn him that if he runs away from you again, he will have to sit in the cart. The choice is his. If he runs away from you again, he loses his privilege to walk beside you. You scoop him up in a no-

nonsense manner and strap him into the cart, explaining that since he ran away, he will have to stay in the cart for the rest of the shopping. While this course seems less severe, he'll learn more from it than he would from the ban on after-dinner playing because the consequence makes sense. It's literally stopping him from doing the thing you're trying to correct. What in the world do running away in a store and playing outdoors after dinner have to do with one another?

Discipline can be very effective when it is thought of merely as a style of teaching your child what is expected of him. Official punishments do not need to play a part in that. Penelope Leach says,

> Older people, who know how they should behave but do not always want to do so, may sometimes be kept from transgression by its cost—detention for talking in class or getting the car towed for illegal parking. Such considerations don't always work for us though, and they don't ever work for young children because they aren't yet able to weigh future penalties against present impulses. The only sanction that works at all reliably with children under four, or even five, is other people's disapproval. Whatever punishment you may announce when you get angry, it is your anger that punishes . . .

> If you are truly trying to show your child how to behave (rather than paying him back for misbehavior) you will usually do better without formal punishments, especially in these early years, because they will make him less, rather than more, inclined to listen to what you say and try to please you. The effective alternative to punishing children who do wrong so that they feel bad is rewarding children who do right so that they feel good. Your child will learn . . . a great deal from your displeasure when he gets things wrong, but most of all from being praised and congratulated when he behaves as you wish.

Punishments put parents and children in opposite corners of the boxing ring and keep them from working together to solve the problems they're facing. Parents who punish often find that the problem behavior only escalates. The child is angry and does the very thing you hate because you keep doing the thing to him that he hates. If your toddler feels you are on his side, helping him learn to behave better, your strong disapproval of his inappropriate actions will be the best deterrent. Make your expectations clear, remind him of them, and gently correct him when he slips up. You will be amazed at how much cooperation you can get.

98.

Don't confuse "spoiling" with "giving".

Please don't be afraid that you are going to spoil your child by giving him generous amounts of your time, love, and attention; by disciplining him with affectionate understanding instead of with authoritarian punishments; by allowing him to do the things he wants to do; or even by showering him with toys and presents. NONE OF THESE PARENTING PRACTICES WILL HURT YOUR TODDLER AS LONG AS THEY ARE DONE FOR THE RIGHT REASONS.

Fear of spoiling is epidemic in our culture, and rightfully so, but our definition of "spoiled" is all messed up. A child who is spoiled is an unhappy, bratty child who tries to control his parents to his advantage. Spoiled children are no fun to be around and they generally lack self-esteem and self-discipline and therefore grow to become unpleasant teenagers and adults.

But a spoiled child is far more likely to result from a family that *withholds* love and attention than from a family that is generous with it. And a child who has a lot of toys is no more likely to be spoiled than a child who has a few. What matters is how the attention, time, love, and even material belongings find their way into the child's possession. Penelope Leach explains it best,

> Spoiling isn't about indulgence and fun, it's about bullying and blackmail. You can't spoil your child with too much talk, play and laughter, too many smiles and hugs, or even too many presents, provided you give them because you want to. Your child will not get spoiled because you buy candy in the supermarket or 15 birthday gifts. But he may get spoiled if he learns that he can blackmail you into reversing a "no candy" decision by throwing a tantrum in public, or get anything he wants out of you if he goes on and on and on . . . The most "spoiled" child you know may not get much more—may even get less—than most children, but he gets whatever comes his way by bullying it out of his parents against their better judgment. Spoiling is the result of the family balance of power getting out of line.

I was ten years old when my sister was born, so I basically remember her entire upbringing. From her infancy right up through her teenage years, my mother was criticized for spoiling her. Relatives, friends' parents, anyone who had the opportunity to observe our family in action, proclaimed that my sister would one day become a monster because of all the attention that was given her and money that was spent on her. Guess what? My now fully-grown, very successful sister has always been and continues to be the most absolutely lovable and fun person in the world. As far as I can tell, she has never been accused of a single negative trait (and should it ever happen, that accuser will have me to tangle with). Indulgence does not spoil a person as long as it is offered willingly and lovingly.

99.

Listen to your child.

While it may seem obvious, one of the best things you can do to raise a happy toddler is to listen to him. Because toddlers are still basically pretty irrational, parents sometimes discredit their feelings or don't take them seriously when the toddlers are trying to communicate something. In their popular book, *How to Talk So Kids Will Listen and Listen So Kids Will Talk*, Adele Faber and Elaine Mazlish outline steps for listening to children that are appropriate for toddlers as well as older kids.

First, you need to hear what your child is saying. Give him your full attention and keep an open, supportive expression on your face. Then, instead of rushing to solve your child's problem, say, "I see," or "Oh," or something that acknowledges the problem. He may take this opportunity to tell you more. Next, say something to indicate that you understand, while labeling the toddler's feeling. One of the best ways to make a toddler feel comfortable with the full range of his emotions is for him to know that what he feels has a name. If he's sad about wanting something he can't have, give him his wish in fantasy form. Here's an example of a toddler who's been denied his unreasonable request to go swimming when it is almost his bedtime:

> Toddler: "I want to go swimming!"
>
> Parent: "It sounds like you really love to swim."
>
> Toddler: "I want to go swimming right now, in my pool!"
>
> Parent: "It's must be hard to want to do something so much, and have to wait until morning to do it."
>
> Toddler: "I really want to swim."
>
> Parent: "I wish I could make it be morning right now so we could go swimming together!"

Listening in this empathetic way really does help a child to express himself and feel better. Some parents worry that labeling and echoing a child's negative emotions will cause them to escalate, but the reverse is true. A child who hears the words for what he is feeling will feel validated and comforted. Once his inner experience has been understood, he can turn his attention to feeling better.

Adele Faber and Elaine Mazlish say,

> But more important than any words we use is our attitude. If our attitude is not one of compassion, then whatever we say will be experienced by the child as phony or manipulative. It is when our words are infused with real feelings of empathy that they speak directly to a child's heart.

100.

Know your child is good.

What if you knew, beyond any doubt, that your child would completely fulfill your true expectations of him? Whether that prediction makes you feel joyous or terrified says a lot about the psychology behind your parenting practices. If you believe in your child—believe in his innate ability to cooperate, thrive, and achieve—and if you consistently communicate that belief to him, he will rise to the occasion (even if he suffers a few setbacks along the way.)

But if you badger, condemn, and convey a message that you are disappointed in your child, he will continue to disappoint you. Sometimes a leap of faith is required. Even if you feel discouraged right now, make a promise to yourself to celebrate your child's strengths. Repeat "my child is good," like a mantra until you can get yourself to believe it. Until you believe it, he can't. And until he believes it, he can't become it.

Penelope Leach wisely points out,

> There's an irony about small children's behavior: the more worried you are about it and the harder you try to change it, the worse it's liable to get.
>
> That's because children are easiest to live with when adults take a positive approach to their behavior, assuming that they mean well, noticing when they do well, making sure they understand what is wanted of them under different circumstances and rewarding good behavior so as to motivate more of the same. Parents who decide that their children are especially badly behaved, or are told so by relatives and caregivers, risk slipping into a negative way of handling them that's the opposite of all that. Negative discipline focuses on bad behavior, expects it, watches for it, punishes it, so as to motivate change, but gets more—and more and *more* of the same.

If you've been in power struggles, try giving up some of your power. If you've been a strict disciplinarian, try easing up on some of your rules. Remember, if a rule isn't there, he can't be accused of breaking it. Wouldn't it be nice to stop punishing so often, to feel like you and your child were on the same side? Who knows how much more cooperation you might get if you knew, deep down, how very good your child really was?

101.

Love with all your heart.

Parental love is a funny thing. More than any other natural human instinct, it brings out the best in people. Even normally selfish people become giving when their children are in need. The very decision to have a child is one of self-sacrifice, and this complete devotion feels natural and right. Is there any other instance in which giving up most of one's sleep, virtually all of one's free time, and putting on hold one's personal pursuits in order to serve another human being would be considered healthy?

Parental devotion to offspring is an irrefutable law of nature for most mammals. A bird—whose natural instinct is to fly away in the face of danger—will stay and protect her nest if her babies are there. Normally timid animals will become fierce predators when protecting their young. It seems that the survival of many species is dependent upon parental love. And we humans are no different. Your child needs your love just to survive, and the more he receives, the better he will thrive.

Childcare expert Tine Thevenin writes,

> "There are no magic formulas. Rearing a child lovingly does not mean that you will have control over how much happiness she will experience in her teenage or adult years. We must love our children, wholly and fully and unconditionally, but not with the mistaken idea that this will protect them from going astray as teenagers, or that it will cloak us all in such loveliness that no unhappiness, pain, anger, doubt, fear, or distress can ever disturb the equilibrium of our family. We are all subject to influences beyond our control that can create detours, stresses, and unhappiness for which we are ill-prepared. Life is difficult. And love is not a magic wand. But love, and everything it represents, provides the best basis for dealing with life, with all its potential problems. We all need all the love we can get, and especially a mother's inherent love at the very beginning: a love that is nurturing but not

smothering; a love that holds us close but is prepared to let go; a love that is given for the benefit of the child, not for the mother's own benefit."

Tell your toddler how wonderful he is. Let him hear you telling other people the same thing. Some parents will compliment a child, but then, assuming the child isn't listening, say to a neighbor, "He's driving me crazy today. I can't wait to get him into bed." A toddler *will* hear and understand a remark like that. And he's more likely to believe an overheard conversation than a statement the parent makes just to him. A discrepancy will only cause him to mistrust the parent.

So keep your focus on your child's very best traits and spend as much time with him as you possibly can. You'll never look back and say, "I wish I had spent more time at the office," or "I wish I had spent more time watching TV," or "I wish I had spent more time on the tennis court." But if you are spending much of your time at an office, watching TV, or playing tennis, you are spending that time away from your toddler. And it is very likely that you *will* look back and say, "I wish I had spent more time with my child during the period he needed me most."

A happy toddler wears his parents' love like a second skin. He feels it—and feels protected by it—at all times. Because of the security it provides him, he's safe to learn, explore, and grow. Have fun with your toddler during these precious, irreplaceable years. Know him. Laugh with him. Understand him and help him. His happiness depends on these things more than any other factors. You are his world, his comfort, his everything. Love him like there's no tomorrow, and his tomorrows will be forever brighter for it.

Bibliography

Baldwin, Rahima. *You Are Your Child's First Teacher.* Berkely, Calif.: Celestial Arts, 1989.

Bowlby, John. *Attachment & Loss: Attachment.* New York: Basic Books, 1969.

———. *A Secure Base.* New York: Basic Books, 1988.

Brazelton, T. Berry, M.D. *The Essential Reference: Your Child's Emotional and Behavioral Development.* Reading, Mass.: Perseus Books, 1992.

———. *On Becoming a Family.* New York: Delta/Seymour Lawrence, 1981.

———. *To Listen to a Child: Understanding the Normal Problems of Growing Up.* Reading, Mass.: Addison-Wesley, 1984.

T. Berry Brazelton, M.D. and Bert G. Cramer. *The Earliest Relationship.* Reading, Mass: Addison-Wesley, 1990.

Briggs, Dorothy Corkille. *Your Child's Self-Esteem.* New York: Doubleday, 1970.

Bumgarner, Norma Jane. *Mothering Your Nursing Toddler.* Schaumburg, Ill.: La Leche League International, 1994.

Chopra, Deepak. *The Seven Spiritual Laws for Parents: Guiding Your Children to Success and Fulfillment.* New York: Harmony Books/Crown Publishers, 1997.

Crary, Elizabeth. *Without Spanking or Spoiling: A Practical Approach to Toddler and Preschool Guidance.* Seattle, Wash.: Parenting Press, 1993.

Cress, Joseph N. *Peaceful Parenting in a Violent World.* Minneapolis, Minn.: Perspective Publications, 1995.

Cullinan, Bernice E. *Read to Me: Raising kids who love to read.* New York: Scholastic, 1992.

Day, Jennifer. *Creative Visualization With Children.* Boston: Element Books, 1994.

Dyer, Wayne W., Dr. *What Do You Really Want for Your Children?* New York: Avon Books, 1997.

Eisenberg, Arlene, Heidi E. Murkoff, and Sandee E. Hathaway, B.S.N. *What to Expect, the Toddler Years.* New York: Workman Publishing, 1996.

Epstein, Randi. "Questioning the 'Deadline' for Weaning." *The New York Times,* September 21, 1999.

Eyre, Linda and Richard. *Teaching Your Children Joy.* New York: Simon & Schuster, 1980.

Faber, Adele, and Elaine Mazlish. *How to Talk So Kids Will Listen & Listen So Kids Will Talk.* New York: Avon Books, 1980.

Ferber, Richard, M.D. *Solve Your Child's Sleep Problems.* New York: Fireside/Simon & Schuster, 1996.

Fraiberg, Selma H. *Every Child's Birthright: In Defense of Mothering.* New York: Basic Books, 1977.

———. The Magic Years: *Understanding and Handling the Problems of Early Childhood.* New York: Charles Scribner's Sons, 1959.

Friel, John C., Ph.D., and Linda D. Friel, M.A. . . . *The 7 Worst Things Parents Do.* Deerfield Beach, Fla.: Health Communications, 1999.

Gerber, Magda and Allison Johnson. *Your Self-Confident Baby: How to Encourage Your Child's Natural Abilities—from the Very Start.* New York: John Wiley & Sons, 1998.

Greenspan, Stanley, M.D. and Nancy Thorndike Greenspan. *First Feelings: Milestones in the Emotional Development of Your Baby and Child.* New York: Penguin, 1985.

Hanley, Kate, and the Parents of Parent Soup. *The Parent Soup A-to-Z Guide to Your Toddler.* Chicago: Contemporary Books, 1999.

Heller, Sharon, Ph.D. *The Vital Touch: How Intimate Contact with Your Baby Leads to Happier, Healthier Development.* New York: Henry Holt, 1997.

Jaffke, Freya. *Work and Play in Early Childhood.* Hudson, N.Y.: Anthroposophic Press, 1996.

Klaus, Marshall H. and John H. Kennell and Phyllis Klaus. *Bonding: Building the Foundation of Secure Attachment and Independence.* Reading, Mass.: Addison-Wesley, 1995.

Kropp, Paul. *Raising a Reader.* New York: Doubleday, 1993.

La Leche League International. *The Womanly Art of Breastfeeding.* New York: Plume/Penguin, 1991.

Leach, Penelope. *Your Baby and Child: From Birth to Age Five.* New York: Alfred A Knopf, 1998.

Lerner, Harriet, Ph.D. *The Mother Dance.* New York: HarperCollins, 1998.

Levinson, Kathy, Ph.D. *First Aid for Tantrums.* Boca Raton, Fla.: Saturn Press, 1998.

Liedloff, Jean. *The Continuum Concept: In Search of Happiness Lost.* Reading, Mass.: Addison Wesley, 1977.

Marston, Stephanie. *The Magic of Encouragement: Nurturing Your Child's Self-Esteem.* New York: Pocket Books/Simon and Schuster, 1990.

McKenna, James. "Sudden Infant Death Syndrome SIDS: Making Sense of Current Research," *Mothering.* Winter 1996.

Montagu, Ashley. Touching: *The Human Significance of the Skin.* New York: Harper & Row, 1986.

Montessori, Maria. *The Absorbent Mind.* New York: Henry Holt, 1995.

Morgan, Elisa and Carol Kuykendall. *What Every Child Needs.* Grand Rapids, Mich.: Zondervan Publishing House, 1997.

Morris, Desmond. *Intimate Behavior.* New York: Random House, 1971.

Nolte, Dorothy Law and Rachel Harris. *Children Learn What They Live—Parenting to Inspire Values.* New York: Workman Publishing, 1998.

Popper, Adrienne. *Parents Book for the Toddler Years.* New York: Ballantine, 1986.

Rosemond, John. *Making the "Terrible" Twos Terrific!* Kansas City, Mis.: Andrews and McMeel, 1993.

Seabrook, John. "Sleeping With the Baby." *The New Yorker,* November 8, 1999.

Sears, William, M.D., and Martha Sears, R.N. *The Baby Book: Everything You Need to Know About Your Baby from Birth to Age Two.* Boston: Little, Brown, 1993.

——. *The Discipline Book: Everything You Need to Know to Have a Better-Behaved Child—From Birth to Age Ten.* Boston: Little, Brown, 1995.

——. *Nighttime Parenting: How to Get Your Baby and Child to Sleep.* New York: Penguin, 1987.

Shimm, Patricia Henderson with Kate Ballen, *Parenting Your Toddler: An Expert's Guide to the Tough and Tender Years.* Reading, Mass.: Perseus Books , 1998.

Solter, Aletha, Ph.D. Tears and Tantrums: *What to Do When Babies and Children Cry.* Goleta, Calif: Shining Star Press, 1998.

Spock, Benjamin, M.D., *Dr. Spock's Baby and Child Care, Revised and Updated 7th Edition.* New York: Dutton/Penguin Putnam, 1998.

Stoppard, Miriam, M.D., *Complete Baby and Child Care.* New York: Dorling Kindersley, 1998.

Tieger, Paul D. and Barbara Barron-Tieger, *Nurture by Nature: Understand Your Child's Personality Type—And Become a Better Parent.* Boston: Little, Brown, 1997.

Thevenin, Tine, *The Family Bed.* Wayne, N.J.: Avery Publishing Group, 1987.

White, Burton L., *The New First Three Years of Life.* New York: Fireside/Simon and Schuster, 1998.

———. *Raising a Happy, Unspoiled Child.* New York: Fireside/Simon and Schuster, 1994.

Willis, Kay and Maryann Bucknum Brinley, *Are We Having Fun, Yet? The 16 Secrets of Happy Parenting.* New York: Warner Books, 1997.

Ziglar, Zig, *Raising Positive Kids in a Negative World.* New York: Ballantine, 1989.

Index

aggressiveness
    intervening, 96
    overreacting to, 95, 96
    reactions to, 97, 98
anger, understanding, 74
attachment parenting, 14, 15
attention diversion, 35
authoritative action, 2, 86

Ballen, Kate
    aggressiveness, 96
    empathy, 61
    limits, setting, 27
    playdates, 4, 5, 6
    reasons, offering, 48
    siblings, new, 100, 101
    tantrums, 35, 36
    teaching, over-, 9
baths as water therapy, 44
battles, selecting appropriate, 7
behavior
    acceptable group
        behavior, 33
    bully, 99, 100
    correction, 8
    destructive, 69
    limits, establishing, 8
    modification, 21
    parental impact, 29
    positive accentuation, 2
    responding to, 37
    separating behavior from
        child, 37
    substitution, 2
behavior modification
    cause and effect, 57
    destructive behavior, 69
    embarrassing
        comments, 71
    empathy, instilling, 60
    reconnection after time-
        out, 22
    responsibility,
        demonstrating, 59
    strategies, time-out, 22
    substitution of behavior, 3
    television viewing,
        monitoring, 42
    time-out to teach, 21
    voice modulation, 81
    whining, preventing,
        72, 73
    yelling, 41
bonding
    clinginess, 92
    co-sleeping. see co-
        sleeping
    everyday activities,
        toddler as part of, 31
    goodness of your
        child, 119
    help, requests of toddler
        to, 82
    listening to your
        child, 117
    nursing. see nursing
    people, with, 14
    reading time, 104
    security, instilling, 13
    separation, 24
    siblings, new, 100
    spoiling, 116
boundaries
    establishing, 26, 27, 28
    testing, 27
bully behavior, 99, 100

cause and effect methodology,
    57, 91
choices, offering, 2
classes, readiness for, 8, 9
clinginess, 92, 93
communication
    boundaries,
        establishing, 26
    choices, offering, 2

directions, giving, 38
listening to your
    child, 117
lying, 11
praising, parental, 79
reconnection after time-
    out, 22
switching activities, prior
    to, 77
telephone conversations,
    during, 40
understanding their
    words, 9
voice modulation, 81
whining, preventing, 72
yelling, 41
compliments, teaching to give
    and receive, 85
consistency, 90
control, relinquishing, 66, 67
co-sleeping
    benefits, 13, 14
    Ferber, Dr. Richard, 17
    options, 18
    security establishment, 13
    statistics, misleading,
        15, 16
creating books about your
    toddler, 108, 109
creativity, opportunities for, 39
crying, 25, 26

daily routine, including
    toddler in, 31, 32
destructive behavior,
    correcting, 69
determination, 34
diaper changing distractions,
    64, 65
directions, giving, 38
discipline
    aggressiveness, 95, 97
    alternatives, 22
    approaches, 115
    cause and effect, 57
    fear, instilling, 46
    guidelines, establishing, 28
    politeness during, 87
    reaction routine,
        establishing, 42
    reasons, offering, 47
    repetitive actions, 88
    responsibility,
        demonstrating, 59
    strategies, situational, 23
    testing, expect, 90
    time-out. *see* time-out
    unified front
        presentation, 27
    yelling. *see* yelling
distractions
    diaper changing,
        during, 64
    nail clipping, during, 62

songs and games, make
    up, 61
songs and games use,
    61–66
whining, 73
diversion, attention, 35
dressing oneself, encouraging
    independence while,
    84, 85
duplication, toy, 6

egocentrism, 1, 11, 12
embarrassing comments,
    coping with, 71, 72
empathy, introducing, 60, 61
errands and activities with
    toddlers, 31–32

fears
    childhood, 93
    instilling, 46
    overcoming, 94, 95
Ferber, Dr. Richard, 17
frustration tolerance,
    developing, 1

Gartner, Dr. Lawrence M., 19
grocery shopping as an
    adventure and teaching
    tool, 52, 53
grooming
    hair cut, preparing for
        first, 67

nail-clipping, 62
songs and games while
distracting, 61
teeth brushing, 45
group behavior, acceptable, 33
guns for play toys, avoiding,
50, 51

haircut, preparing for first,
67, 68
happiness, recognizing, 59, 60
helpfulness, accepting your
toddlers offers of, 82

imaginative play, indulging
in, 75, 76
imitation
parental, 29
playdates, effect of, 4
independence
cultural emphasis on, 13
dressing, while, 84, 85
encouraging, 49
fostering, 13
sleep, 17, 18
intimacy, childrens need
for, 15

joy, recognizing, 59, 60
justification to requests, 47

Kropp, Paul, 107
Kutner, Lawrence

lying and magical
thinking, 11, 12
preschool, selecting,
110, 111
understanding of their
words, toddlers, 9, 10
yelling, 41

laundry as an activity, 83
Leach, Penelope
bribery, 58
guns and aggressive play,
toy, 51, 52
limits, setting, 8, 28
punishment, 47
reasons, offering, 47, 48
spoiling, 116
television viewing, 43
learning, pushing toddlers
towards, 8, 9
library trip advantages,
106, 107
limits, testing, 27
listening to your toddler,
117, 118
lying, 11

magical thinking of toddlers,
11, 12
manners
compliments, giving and
receiving, 85

embarrassing
comments, 71
mealtimes, 70
politeness, 30
voice modulation, 81
mealtimes, 70, 71

nail clipping, songs and
games used as
distractions, 62, 63
Newton, Niles, 20
nursing
La Leche, 20
Newton, Niles, 20
pressure to wean,
societal, 19
reducing feedings, 19

operant conditioning, 102,
103, 104

parallel play, 4
parenting pitfalls
discipline, threats of, 46
over-teaching, 8
reasons, offering, 47
television viewing,
monitoring, 42
time-outs, 21
patience in toddlers world,
30, 31
personal time, recognizing
need for, 25

playdates, 4
    activities, 5
    imitation effect, 4
    parallel play, 4
    respect, introducing
    sharing, introducing, 4
politeness, 30, 87
powerlessness, underscoring, 2
praise, offering parental,
    79, 80
preschool
    selection, 110, 111
    transition, 111
    visiting, 112
pull-ups and put-downs
    methodology, 80
put-downs and pull-ups
    methodology, 80

readiness for classes, 8
reading
    importance, 104, 105
    preparing toddler for, 107
reasons to requests, giving, 47
reconnection after time-out is
    completed, 22
respect, teaching, 4
responsibility, teaching, 59
restrictions, imposing, 26,
    27, 28
Rosemond, John
    aggressiveness, 95
    sharing, 6

simplicity of
    discussions, 86
testing, expect, 90
toilet training, 56

Seabrook, John, 18, 19
Sears, Dr. William, 29
    authoritarianism, 67
    co-sleeping, 13, 14
    fears, accepting, 94
    mealtimes, 70, 71
    whining, distractions
        during, 74, 75
self-esteem
    choices, offering, 2
    compliments, giving and
        receiving, 85
    creativity, encouraging, 39
    dressing, encourage
        while, 84
    help, accepting your
        toddlers, 49
    judging behavior, not
        child, 37
    listening to your child, 117
    praise, parental, 79
    toilet training. *see* toilet
        training
    yelling, 41
separation from toddler, 24
sharing
    duplication, toy, 6
    expectations, parental, 6

introducing, 5
playdates, setting, 4
readiness, 6
teaching, 4, 5, 6
Shimm, Patricia Henderson
    aggressiveness, 96
    empathy, 61
    limits, setting, 27
    playdates, 4, 5
    reasons, offering, 48
    sharing, 6
    siblings, new, 100, 101
    tantrums, 35, 36
    teaching, over-, 9
siblings, new, 100, 101
Skinner box, 102
sleep. *see also* co-sleeping
    arrangements, 16, 17
    co-sleeping. *see* co-
        sleeping
    fears, coping with your
        childs, 94
    security, instilling, 13
songs and games used as
    distractions, 61–65
speech development, 9, 10,
    78, 79
spoiling, 116, 117
sponge effect, 29
strategic opportunity
    method, 89
stubbornness, 34
substitution, behavior, 2

talking. *see* speech
development
tantrums
discussion with toddler, 37
expressions, behavioral, 35
frequency, 1
inevitability, 1
reactions, parental, 35
reconnection after, 36
teaching
responsibility, 59
thinking for oneself, 47
teeth brushing, establishing,
45, 46
telephone conversations, 40

television viewing,
monitoring, 42, 43
testing parents, 90
thinking for oneself, 47
time-outs
application, 20
behavior modification, 21
reconnection after time-
out is completed, 22
rules, 21
toilet training
accidents, 57
method determination, 55
selection, potty, 54, 55
signs, readiness, 53
suggestions, 56

transition between activities,
77, 78
voice modulation, 81
water therapy, 44
whining, preventing, 72,
73, 74
why, asking, 91
writing, preparing toddler
for, 108

yelling
effectiveness, 41
impact on toddlers, 41
misinterpretation, 41

Also by Lisa McCourt:

101 Ways to Raise a

Happy Baby

available at bookstores

everywhere

or
Contact Department CS at the following address:
NTC/Contemporary Publishing Group
4255 West Touhy Avenue
Lincolnwood, IL 60712-1975
1-800-323-4900

PEABODY INSTITUTE
LIBRARY
DANVERS, MASS.